50
Early Childhood Literacy Strategies

50
Early Childhood Literacy Strategies

Third Edition

JANICE J. BEATY
Elmira College, Emerita

PEARSON

Boston   Columbus   Indianapolis   New York   San Francisco   Upper Saddle River   Amsterdam
Cape Town   Dubai   London   Madrid   Milan   Munich   Paris   Montreal   Toronto
Delhi   Mexico City   São Paulo   Sydney   Hong Kong   Seoul   Singapore   Taipei   Tokyo

Vice President, Editor-in-Chief: Aurora Martínez Ramos
Associate Sponsoring Editor: Barbara Strickland
Editorial Assistant: Michelle Hochberg
Executive Marketing Manager: Krista Clark
Production Manager: Maggie Brobeck
Editorial Production and Composition Service: Dhanya Ramesh, Jouve
Manager, Central Design: Jayne Conte
Cover Designer: Karen Salzbach

Credits and acknowledgments borrowed from other sources and reproduced, with permission, in this textbook appear here.

Cover photo: Paul Bradbury/Alamy.
Interior photos by Janice J. Beaty.

Library of Congress Cataloging-in-Publication Data

Beaty, Janice J.
  50 early childhood literacy strategies / Janice J. Beaty. — 3rd ed.
     p. cm.
  Includes bibliographical references.
  ISBN 978-0-13-269007-2
  1. Language arts (Early childhood)   2. Early childhood education—Activity programs.   3. Picture books for children.   I. Title.   II. Title: Fifty early childhood literacy strategies.
  LB1139.5.L35B42 2013
  372.6—dc23

                                                                                        2011048328

ISBN 10: 0-13-269007-1
ISBN 13: 978-0-13-269007-2

About the Author

Janice J. Beaty, Professor Emerita, Elmira College, Elmira, New York, is a full-time writer of early childhood college textbooks and a consultant and trainer in early childhood education from her home in Cape Coral, Florida. Some of her Pearson textbooks include *Skills for Preschool Teachers,* Ninth Edition; *Observing Development of the Young Child,* Seventh Edition; *Early Literacy in Preschool and Kindergarten,* Third Edition (with Linda Pratt); and *50 Early Childhood Guidance Strategies* (also in Chinese). Dr. Beaty is also engaged in training Foster Grandparents to work with young children in Columbia, Missouri, and Cottonwood, Arizona.

Contents

Children's Picture Books
(Listed or Described)

*Multicultural

Aaaarrgghh! Spider! (Monks, L., 2004)
Abuela (Dorros, A., 1991)*
Abuelita Full of Life (Costales, A., 2007)*
Alligator Arrived with Apples (Dragonwagon, C., 1986)
Alligator Baby (Munsch, R., 1997)
Alphabet under Construction (Fleming, D., 2003)
Amazing Grace (Hoffman, M., 1991)*
Art (McDonnell, P., 2006)
Art and Max (Wiesner, D., 2010)
B Is for Bulldozer: A Construction ABC (Sobel, S., 2003)
Bats at the Library (Lies, B., 2008)
Bats at the Beach (Lies, B., 2006)
Bebé Goes Shopping (Elya, S., 2006)*
Bee-bim Bop! (Park, S., 2005)*
Big Bug Surprise (Gran, J., 2007)
Block City (Stevenson, R.L., 2005)
Boo! Made You Jump! (Child, L., 2007)
Boo to You! (Ehlert, L., 2009)
Boom Boom Go Away! (Geringer, L., 2010)
Born to Read (Sierra, J., 2008)
Bounce (Cronin, D., 2007)
Brown Bear, Brown Bear, What Do You See? (Martin, B. & Carle, E., 1990)
Bunny Cakes (Wells, R., 1997)
But Excuse Me That Is My Book (Child, L., 2005)
Can You Say Peace? (Katz, K., 2006)*
Captain Cheech (Marin, C., 2008)*
Carlo Likes Reading (Spanyol, J., 2001)
Carlos and the Squash Plant (Stevens, J., 1993)*
Carolina's Story (Rathmell, D., 2005)
Chalk (Thomson, B., 2010)
Chick 'n' Pug (Sattler, J., 2010)
Chicka Chicka Boom Boom (Martin, B. & Archambault, J., 1989)
Clarabella's Teeth (Vrombaut, A., 2003)
Click, Clack, Moo: Cows That Type (Cronin, D., 2000)
Clink, Clank, Clunk! (Aroner, M., 2006)
Clip Clop (Smee, N., 2006)
Crab Moon (Horowitz, R., 2000)
Diary of a Spider (Cronin, D., 2005)
Diary of a Worm (Cronin, D., 2003)
Dinosaurumpus! (Mitton, T., 2002)
Doctor Ted (Beaty, A., 2008)
Do You Do a Didgeridoo? (Page, N., 2008)
Down by the Cool of the Pool (Mitton, T., 2000)

Dragonfly Kites (Highway, T., 2002)
Drat That Fat Cat! (Thompson, P., 2003)
Duck in the Truck (Alborough, J., 1999)
Duck on a Bike (Shannon, D., 2003)
Duck Soup (Urbanovic, J., 2009)
Eating the Alphabet (Ehlert, L., 1989)
Eleanor, Ellatony, Ellencake, and Me (Rubin, C., 2003)
The Empanadas That Abuela Made (Bertrand, D., 2003)*
Fast Food (Freyman, S., & Elffers, J., 2006)
Fire! Fire! Said Mrs. McGuire (Martin, B., 2006)
Flower Garden (Bunting, E., 1994)*
Five Little Monkeys Jumping on the Bed (Christelow, E., 1989)
Friday My Radio Flyer Flew (Pullen, Z., 2008)
Froggy Goes to the Doctor (London, J., 2002)
Gathering the Sun: An Alphabet in Spanish and English (Ada, A. F., 1997)*
Giggle, Giggle, Quack (Cronin, D., 2002)
Gingerbread Cowboy, The (Squires, J., 2006)
Giraffes Can't Dance (Andreae, G., 1999)
Goodnight Moon (Brown, M., 1947)
Green Eggs and Ham (Seuss, Dr., 1988)
Grumpy Gloria (Dewdney, A., 2006)
Gumption (Broach, E., 2010)
Handa's Surprise (Browne, E., 1994)*
Harry and the Dinosaurs Go to School (Whybrow, I., 2006)
Harry and the Dinosaurs Say "Raahh!" (Whybrow, I., 2001)
Hedgie Blasts Off! (Brett, J., 2006)
Henry Builds a Cabin (Johnson, D., 2002)
Hoops with Swoopes (Kuklin, S., 2001)
The House in the Night (Swanson, S., 2008)
How Do Dinosaurs Get Well Soon? (Yolen, J., 2003)*
How Do Dinosaurs Say Good Night? (Yolen, J., 2000)*
Hush! A Thai Lullaby (Ho, H., 1996)*
I Am Not Sleepy and I Will Not Go to Bed (Child, L., 2001)
I Am Too Absolutely Small for School (Child, L., 2004)
I Can Do Anything (Child, L., 2008)
I Can Be Anything (Spinelli, J., 2010)
I Can Do It Too! (Baicker, K., 2003)*
I Like Myself (Beaumont, K., 2004)
I Love Bugs! (Dodd, E., 2010)

Educational Supply Companies

Lakeshore Learning Materials
2695 E. Dominguez St.
Carson, CA 9081
(1-800-778-4456)
www.lakeshorelearning.com

Childcraft Education Corporation
PO Box 3229
Lancaster, PA 17604
(1-800-631-5652)
www.childcraft.com

Constructive Playthings
13201 Arrington Rd.
Grandview, MO 64030
(1-800-448-4115)
www.cptoys.com

Demco Reading Enrichment
PO Box 7488
Madison, WI 53707
(1-800-356-1200)
www.demco.com

Scholastic, Inc.
2931 E. McCarty St.
Jefferson City, MO 65101
(1-800-724-6527)
www.scholastic.com

Preface

Teaching literacy to young children is a new addition to the curriculum of many early childhood programs. *50 Early Childhood Literacy Strategies,* Third Edition, presents an easy-to-use, easy-to-understand approach involving young children's own emergence into the world of speaking and listening, reading, and writing. Teachers and student teachers quickly learn what picture books and activities to use with children, how to use them, and how children can benefit from their use. They also learn what to expect as young children's writing emerges from scribbles, to pictures, to real words. And finally they are able to come to grips with the concept of *emergent literacy* as it appears in preschool children and evolves into *conventional literacy* as it is taught in elementary school.

Our ideas on how children learn to read and write are continuing to change as advances in neuroscience give us new understandings of the human brain and reading research uncovers core skills necessary for how children learn to read. This text takes advantage of this new knowledge by presenting strategies that speak to the way children learn. These strategies are tied to the ordinary contents and activities of the early childhood classroom; that is, books, blocks, chalk, crayons, computers, dolls, dramatic play, easel painting, finger painting, puppets, chanting, singing, and storytelling. But the contents and activities are given a "literacy twist" that helps teachers set them up for children's development of early reading, writing, listening, and speaking.

Each strategy begins with a literacy concept that briefly but concisely explains the topic. At the heart of each strategy are the practical literacy activities to be used with children, often involving hands-on story activities, drawing, writing, singing, and pretending with character cutouts, toy animals, and the children themselves. The theme throughout the text focuses on *words*: hearing words, speaking words, writing words, and reading words—the basis of early literacy. At the same time, the strategies focus on *children* and what they can do to develop these literacy skills. There are more than 50 ways.

Each young child comes to the literacy table as an individual who joins the feast at different times, at different levels, and with an appetite appropriate only to him- or herself. With 50 different dishes set before them, children and teachers alike can pick and choose what works best for them. Good appetite!

Key Features

- Strategies are arranged in three parts for easy selection: Part I, Children's Speaking/Listening; Part II, Children's Writing; and Part III, Children's Reading.

- Most of the strategies are tied to children's picture books at the early childhood level. Within the strategies, 178 of the finest books have been selected and described or listed.

- The activities described have been chosen as models for your easy use, as well as to emulate with your own ideas. These activities have been used by the author or by teachers she has observed.

- Assessment of children's literacy progress can be partially accomplished with the following developmental checklists: Early Childhood Writing Behaviors, Reading Behaviors, Speaking Behaviors, and Caption Writing Progress, along with observation of children, interviews, and children's products.

New to This Edition

As more early childhood programs adopt early reading activities and more research focuses on how children develop literacy skills, this text shifts its own priorities and updates its own information. Some of the changes include the following:

- New Strategies added:
  4: Listening Center
  10: Vocabulary Development
  21: Taking Dictation
  27: Dual Language Learners' Writing

- How to teach children to "listen with intent"
- Why "phonological awareness" is important, and how children develop it
- How dual language learners often develop *interlanguage* when learning to speak English
- How dual language writers reconstruct the written system in order to make it their own
- How children learn to recognize "word-meaning clues" in building their vocabularies
- How kindergarten reading is different from preschool reading
- Strategies updated with 64 new references
- Among the 178 books described, 77 new picture books are included
- All new photographs by the author of children engaged in literacy activities within the past year; also all new children's art
- An appendix containing 26 pertinent websites

Using This Book

50 Early Childhood Literacy Strategies, Third Edition, can be used by itself as a handy activities book by teachers, student teachers, and volunteers. It can also be used in any early childhood methods and materials course, children's literature or language course, or any reading or literacy course. College students especially appreciate activity books like this for use in their student teaching or practicum experiences. In addition, it can be used as a supplement to early literacy textbooks such as the author's *Early Literacy in Preschool and Kindergarten: A Multicultural Perspective*, Third Edition (with Linda Pratt), or other textbooks by the author such as *Skills for Preschool Teachers*, Ninth Edition, or *Observing Development of the Young Child,* Seventh Edition. It is not necessary to read the book from beginning to end in chapter sequence. The strategies can be selected and used in any order helpful to the teacher.

CourseSmart eBook and other eBook Options Available

CourseSmart is an exciting new choice for purchasing this book. As an alternative to purchasing the printed book, you may purchase an electronic version of the same content via CourseSmart for reading on PC, Mac, as well as Android devices, iPad, iPhone, and iPod Touch with CourseSmart Apps. With a CourseSmart eBook, readers can search the text, make notes online, and bookmark important passages for later review. For more information or to purchase access to the CourseSmart eBook, visit http://www.coursesmart.com. Also look for availability of this book on a number of other eBook devices and platforms.

Acknowledgments

I want to thank my new editor, Aurora Martinez, for her help and support; Dr. Linda Pratt, Executive Director of the Elmira College education program, for being the "godmother" of this text; Ann Gilchrist, Executive Director of the Central Missouri Foster Grandparents program, for allowing me to work with and film the wonderful children, teachers, and foster grandparents working in Tiger Paws Head Start and Trinity Lutheran Child Learning Center in Columbia, with thanks also to its director, Gail Schuster.

I also wish to thank the following programs and their impressive children artists for sharing their exciting art: Head Start Programs in Jefferson City, Perryville, Fredericktown, Anderson, Maysville, Springfield, Excelsior Springs, Cape Girardeau, Kansas City, Adrian, Chamois, Cassville, Branson, Republic, Marble Hill, Mineral Point, and Carrolton, Missouri contributed. And to Elaine West, executive director of the Missouri Association for Community Action, Inc., for allowing me to use the outstanding children's art created in these Head Start classes for the annual MACA calendar. Finally, many thanks are extended to the following reviewers: Marlene Cousens, Yakima Valley Community College; Erin Kay Jurand, American University; Lee Anne Larsen, Maine Department of Education; and Lisa Norris, Iowa State University.

50
Early Childhood Literacy Strategies

Part 1

Children's Speaking/Listening

 **Emergent Literacy**

CONCEPT

Emergent literacy is the overall process through which young children learn to read and write in a natural, self-discovery manner that begins at birth and can continue through the preschool years and into the early elementary years with proper support. Children then continue learning these skills by being taught in a conventional manner. Literacy itself encompasses the skills of speaking, listening, reading, and writing.

Circuits in the brain are already set up for infants, toddlers, and preschoolers to emerge naturally into speaking the language(s) they hear spoken around them. Children do not have to be taught language. But learning to read and write must be converted by young children into this language module of the brain by hearing and seeing language in its spoken and written forms. In other words, speaking is natural, but reading and writing are not. They have to be acquired. They can either emerge naturally if the circumstances are right or they have to be taught, or both.

Some young children seem to learn to read on their own from stories read to them, from computer programs they use, and from the printed material they see around them. But most children need adult assistance to involve them in appropriate literacy activities and to help them interpret what they are seeing and hearing. The natural emergence process occurs when children discover how to read and write on their own from these activities. The conventional process of learning to read and write occurs when teachers take charge and have children follow their directions. During the preschool years,

Children can emerge into reading on their own with appropriate books and support.

Listening. Sharpen children's abilities to attend to sounds.

Rhyming. Focus children's attention on ending sounds of words.

Words and sentences. Develop children's awareness that language is made up of strings of words.

Syllables. Develop children's ability to separate words into syllables.

Sound matching. Ask children which words start with a specific sound.

Initial and final sounds. Ask children which sound occurs at the beginning or at the end of a word.

Blending. Ask children to combine sounds to form words.

Segmentation. Ask children to break up words into sounds.

Phonemic manipulation. Ask children to say words with or without certain sounds.

FIGURE 1–1   SBRR Direct Instructional Activities.

both processes are in play, but it is emergent literacy that should be encouraged whenever possible. Preschool children may function at either or both of these levels. If children are able to develop skills as they engage in literacy activities on their own, they are exhibiting emergent literacy. If children are taught by the teacher, they are learning through conventional teaching.

In recent years experimental research has swung away from emergent literacy and has identified a core of skills that young children need to master to become proficient readers and writers (see Figure 1–1). These strategies, known as *scientifically based reading research* (SBRR), focus on the visual and auditory processing aspects of literacy as *taught by a teacher,* whereas emergent literacy focuses on the social and meaning-based aspects of literacy *as they emerge* with a teacher's support. Many early childhood specialists now feel that a combination of the two strategies is the most effective early literacy instruction. Vukelich and Christie (2009) have developed eight basic principles of effective early literacy instruction by combining emergent literacy and SBRR. The 50 early literacy strategies included in this text expand on these ideas (see Figure 1–2).

1. **Early language and literacy focus:** Oral language; alphabet knowledge; phonological awareness; concepts of print

2. **Oral language foundation:** Have rich conversations; topical vocabularies; photo narration

3. **Storybook reading:** In large and small groups; with individuals; a variety of books; children participating

4. **Planned classroom environment:** Print-rich environment; well-stocked library; reading center; writing center; listening center

5. **Emergent reading and writing:** Investigate books that are read; read lists, schedules, calendars; incorporate literacy into play; use shared reading and shared writing

6. **Direct instruction used carefully:** In shared reading, shared writing; in rhymes, songs, games

7. **Help parents support children's language, reading, and writing:** Connect with significant people; stress importance of home help; send books and activities home

8. **Assessment guided by standards:** State research-based guidelines

FIGURE 1–2   Balanced Early Literacy Instruction.

Activities

1. Make a list of all the speaking activities involving the children and you for one week. Be sure to include types of child-child communication and teacher-child communication. Include story reading, storytelling, dramatic play, and block play. Include any speaking activities with toy phones, microphones, tape recorders, or other specific speaking setups. Decide which of these activities promotes emergent literacy.

2. Make a list of all the listening activities involving the children. Include story reading and storytelling, tape, CD, or video listening, music, word sounds, animal sounds, and other specific listening activities. Decide which of these activities promotes emergent literacy.

3. Make a list of all the reading activities involving children. Tell how each activity promotes specific emergent reading skills.

4. Make a list of all the writing activities involving the children. Tell how each activity promotes specific emergent writing skills. Collect writing artifacts made by the children and tell how each demonstrates the progress of the child. Be sure to include art.

5. Compare your results in these four areas with the charts in Figures 1–1 and 1–2. Have you included in your curriculum all of the activities listed in Figure 1–2? Are there areas where you can improve your program?

SUGGESTED READINGS

Beaty, J. J., & Pratt, L. (2011). *Early literacy in preschool and kindergarten: A multicultural perspective.* 3rd ed. Boston: Pearson.

Vukelich, C., & Christie, J. (2009). *Building a foundation for preschool literacy: Effective instruction for children's reading and writing development.* 2nd ed. Newark, DE: International Reading Association.

2 Speaking Words

CONCEPT 1

Literacy for young children begins with speaking and listening to words and sentences. Roskos, Tabors, and Lenhart (2009) tell us that oral language is the foundation of learning to read and write. For children to become literate, they need to hear language spoken around them. They need to speak it themselves. Learning the sounds of language is the key to their later recognition of written words and letters. Teachers need to spend time daily talking to individuals about things they find interesting, and motivating other children to join in the talk.

Roskos et al. also point out that from age 3 onward "children should encounter and explore at least two to four new words each day" (p. 1). When teachers use new words, they need to point them out. When children use new words, they need to be recognized and commended.

Do not correct mispronounced words. Young children need to feel confident in their early stages of language acquisition. They will hear you pronouncing the words correctly and eventually copy you. Young children learn best through play. Be sure to include many word games on a daily basis. Small groups work best so that no one needs to wait long for a turn. Make *spoken words* the core of your literacy curriculum.

Children can learn to express their feelings in words.

Activities 1

1. "Pack Your Backpack" game. Sit in a circle with a small group and an empty backpack. Say: "I'm packing my backpack for a trip to Mars, and in it I put a _____." Make your pretend item something the children will remember, such as "a gorilla" or "a motorcycle." Then pass the backpack to the child next to you, having her repeat what you said and add a pretend something of her own. Keep the game going as long as the children can keep remembering the items and adding new things. Make positive comments on words the children use (e.g., "A snorkel! Isn't that wonderful? Josh is going to take a snorkel to Mars! Can you tell the others what a snorkel is?").

2. "Follow-the-Leader Word Fishing." Lead the class around the room, one behind the other, pretending you are the captain of a fishing boat. Use an aquarium fish net if you have one. As you walk say: "Words, words, words, words. I'm going to catch a word." As you go by the block center, pick up a toy locomotive (or bulldozer) in your net and say, "I've caught a locomotive, a locomotive, a locomotive." Have everyone behind you repeat the word out loud until you put the locomotive on a table and catch a new word, perhaps a toy dinosaur, saying: "I've caught a tyrannosaurus, a tyrannosaurus, a tyrannosaurus." When the children catch on, give the next child behind you the net and a chance to catch a new word. After everyone has had a turn, hold up each of the caught items on the table for the children to name. (This is a favorite game, by the way.)

CONCEPT 2

Brain imagery by neuroscientists has discovered that "reading relies on brain circuits already in place for language" (Shaywitz, 2003, p. 67). Teachers need to encourage children to use these language circuits even before circuits for reading are in place. Thus, young children need to become aware of the sounds of words and use them repeatedly before they encounter written words.

Activities 2

Wonderful word sounds can be found in books that tell *cumulative stories* where words must be repeated over and over each time a new object is added. You can read the story while children join in with the repeated words.

*1. Read **The Empanadas that Abuela Made** (Bertand, D. G., 2003, Houston: Pinata Books, bilingual).* Each ingredient for the pumpkin tarts is added one by one by grandchildren, grandfather, dog, cousins, and family, as your listeners repeat the verse on every page. Do it in Spanish and your children will soon be speaking words in that language. Follow the recipe on the last page to make your own tarts.

*2. Read **The Gingerbread Cowboy** (Squires, J., 2006, New York: Geringer).* The gingerbread cowboy jumps out of the rancher's oven and runs away from a horned lizard, a roadrunner, a band of javelinas, a herd of long-horned cattle, and finally some hungry cowboys until he is "rescued" by—yes, a coyote. Children love to repeat "giddyup, giddyup as fast as you can," and laugh at the pictures as you flip the pages.

*3. Read **The Runaway Tortilla** (Kimmel, E. A., 2000, Delray Beach FL: Winslow).* It rolls away from two horned toads scampering, three donkeys trotting, four jackrabbits leaping, five rattlesnakes hissing, and six buckaroos loping along until Señor Coyote also fools it into rolling into his mouth.

*4. Read **Roar of a Snore** (Arnold, M. D., 2006, New York: Dial Press).* A snore wakes up Jack, so he goes searching for who is making it, waking up Blue, who wakes up Mama Gwyn, Baby Sue, Papa Ben, Josie Jo, Jenny Lynn, and all the critters in the barn, who all go searching. Children repeat the names of all the searchers every time a new one is added.

CONCEPT 3

Other words children need to know and say out loud are emotional words from times when they are angry. The more emotional the word, the more meaningful it becomes to a child. Having children repeat emotional words aloud helps them to diffuse the emotion, but they remember the word and its sound. Children need to know as many words as possible to describe their feelings. They may not know many words that express anger. You can help by using some of the words in Figure 2–1 and helping children to say them aloud when upsetting situations occur. Feeling words can help diffuse a situation if a child says, "I'm mad!" instead of acting out the anger by yelling or hitting. These words not only help them express their anger but also help them feel better. Children like to use big words like these.

Activities 3

Reading books about becoming angry also helps. If you cannot acquire any of these books from a library or bookstore, make up your own anger stories or bring in a pot and have a "mean soup day," shouting angry words into the pot while stirring out the emotion.

1. Read **Mean Soup** (Everitt, B., 1992, San Diego: Harcourt). Horace has a bad day at school, so his mother puts on a pot of water to make mean soup. For the ingredients, they shout all their troubles away into the pot until they end up smiling. You can bring in a pot for pretend mean soup and have upset children shout and stir words into it that tell how they feel until they feel good again.

2. Read **Sometimes I'm Bombaloo** (Vail, R., 2002, New York: Scholastic). Katie Honor is usually a good kid, but sometimes when things do not go right she becomes Bombaloo, who shows her teeth, makes fierce noises instead of words, and throws things. What words would your children use if they were Bombaloo?

3. Read **When Sophie Gets Angry—Really, Really Angry** (Bang, M., 1999, New York: Blue Sky Press). When her sister snatches her toy gorilla away, Sophie gets so angry she roars a red roar like a volcano. What anger words can your children roar?

4. Read **Grumpy Gloria** (Dewdney, A., 2006, New York: Viking Press). Here is a wonderfully funny book about a pet dog, Gloria, and all the grumpy words she feels—snort, scowl, crabby, grouchy—when the children try to have fun with her.

Mad	Irritated
Angry	Incensed
Crabby	Exasperated
Cross	Boiling
Upset	Fuming
Annoyed	Furious
Disgusted	Enraged
Grumpy	Infuriated

FIGURE 2–1   Feeling Words to Express Anger.

SUGGESTED READINGS

Kalmar, K. (2008). Let's give children something to talk about! Oral language and preschool literacy. *Young Children, 63*(1), 88–92.

Roskos, K. A., Tabors, P. O., & Lenhart, L. A. (2009). *Oral language and early literacy in preschool: Talking, reading, and writing.* 2nd ed. Newark, DE: International Reading Association.

Shaywitz, S. (2003). *Overcoming dyslexia: A new and complete science-based program for reading problems at any level.* New York: Knopf.

Vance, E., & Weaver, P. J. (2003). Words to describe feelings. *Young Children, 58*(4), 45.

Listening with Intent

CONCEPT 1

Children learn to speak by hearing words spoken around them, just as they learn to read in part by hearing stories read to them. But to hear these words, children need to listen. To understand these words, children need to listen with intent. Jalongo (2008) tells us: "Listening is the process of taking in information through the sense of hearing and making meaning in the mind" (p. 12). Listening with intent is the process of paying attention to what is being said and trying to interpret it—to give it meaning.

Young children need to learn to listen to the speaking going on around them. How do they do it? First, they need to be able to hear clearly. If they pay little attention to what you are saying to them or do not seem to hear what you say, they may need to be screened for hearing impairments or attention deficits. Do not wait until they enter elementary school. The earlier such deficits can be identified, the sooner they can be corrected.

Second, children need to be able to identify words being spoken. Every early childhood classroom is full of talking and the noise of boisterous children at work and play. Still, you should be able to hear what the children are saying without raising your voice. A child should be able to hear you without shushing others around. If you hear only loud noises and shouting or if you spend too much time trying to quiet the children, you may need to soundproof the environment.

Soundproof the Environment

To be able to listen to and hear what you are saying, children need to filter out other extraneous sounds, noises, and distractions around them. Look at the classroom itself to see what can be done to cut down the noise. It can be converted into an enjoyable physical listening environment in a number of ways without seriously disrupting children in their normal activities. (See Figure 3–1.)

Talk to each child on a toy phone. Listen with intent to what he says. Is he listening carefully to you?

- Use acoustical ceiling tiles.

- Hang cloth mobiles from ceiling.

- Use curtains or drapes at windows.

- Use cork panels and bulletin boards.

- Use colorful cloth on room dividers.

- Use fabric-wrapped fiberboard on walls.

- Have fluffy area rugs on carpet.

- Use floor pillows, cloth beanbag chairs.

- Place thick towels under pounding stumps.

- Have cloth dolls, puppets, stuffed animals.

FIGURE 3–1   Physical Listening Environment.

Activities 1

1. Start with the ceiling. What do you see when you look up? Is the ceiling smooth and flat? You may need to recommend that acoustical ceiling tiles be installed. Hanging cloth mobiles from the ceiling also helps.

2. Next, look at walls and windows. Various types of wall coverings can be used to absorb noise. Curtains or drapes at windows absorb more noise than blinds or shutters. Corkboards for bulletin boards and cork panels in learning centers are excellent sound absorbers. Colored burlap or similar material can be fastened to backs of room dividers or used for wall hangings. Any kind of cloth material absorbs sound. Fabric-wrapped fiberboard can cover an entire wall.

3. What about floor coverings? Placing fluffy area rugs here and there on the carpeting provides sound absorption. Floor pillows, cloth beanbag chairs, and floor rockers also help. If you are teaching in a program without funds for expensive materials, you can cut apart large cardboard cartons or delivery cases, cover them with colorful cloth or hang them with colorful bath towels and use them for room dividers. Place a thick towel under pounding stumps in the woodworking center. Think "cloth" when ordering materials: cloth dolls, book characters, and puppets; stuffed animals, pillows, and dress-up clothes. What else can be covered with absorbent material?

CONCEPT 2

Teach Children to Listen with Intent

Children can be taught to listen. Attentive listeners become quiet when someone speaks to them. They listen for key words. They wait until the speaker is finished before responding. You can help children listen with intent by talking to each individual in the class every day, using your own listening skills. Keep a list of the children's names handy and check them off each time you speak to an individual. If you miss anyone, be sure to speak to them the next day. What kinds of things might you talk about?

1. Greet each child in the morning, using their names and saying something about their trip to school. Give them a chance to answer. Listen to their answers attentively.

2. Talk to a child on one of the toy phones when you see him near a second phone. Say, "Pick up the phone, Jeremy. Someone wants to talk to you."

3. Talk to a child in each of the learning centers. Say, "Oh, Lily, the colors you are using in your painting are just like the ones in your shirt." Or "Andy, what an interesting building you're making with the unit blocks."

4. Talk to the child next to you at lunch. Say, "I'm glad we're having applesauce today. Apples are my favorite fruit. What about you?"

5. Talk to a child in conflict with another child. Say, "How do you think he feels, Ramon? Look at his face. What does it tell you?"

Children 3 to 5 years old may not understand everything you say. Using some of the following teacher communication behaviors may help children understand:

- Use simple sentences.
- Speak slowly and clearly.
- Vary your tone/expression to emphasize key words.
- Pause between sentences.
- Try to use comments more than questions.

Children can also learn to listen from simple listening games. Include at least one specific listening activity every week for a small group of children in one of the classroom learning centers.

Activities 2

1. Book Center. Read and talk about one of the following books with a listening theme: **Oliver Has Something to Say!** (Edwards, P., 2007, Montreal: Lobster Press); **Polar Bear, Polar Bear, What Do You Hear?** (Martin, B., & Carle, E., 1991, New York: Henry Holt); **The Sound of Day, The Sound of Night** (O'Neill, M., 2003, New York: Farrar, Straus, & Giroux).

2. Block Center. Play a "Who Is Missing?" game. Take out five farm animals (cow, sheep, goat, horse, pig) and have the children say the name of each animal. Put four of the animals in a box. Now, say "Uh-oh, one of the animals is missing. I wonder which one." Have children say names and guess. Play this several times with different animals missing. Then say: "Okay, now build a barn or a corral for these animals so they won't run away." (This game can also be played with jungle animals, zoo animals, or block people.)

3. Art Center. Make animal headbands with ears for each of the animals in the book **Polar Bear, Polar Bear, What Do You Hear?** (polar bear, lion, hippopotamus, flamingo, zebra, boa constrictor, elephant, leopard, peacock, walrus). Children can color the bands like the book animal colors. You can help with the ears. Children can wear the headband of their animal and make its noise as you read. They will need to listen with intent so that they hear the words and come in at the right time.

4. Music Center. Put on a music tape or CD that asks children to listen and follow directions. *Kids in Motion* leads children through the "Tummy Tango" and "Beanbag Boogie." *Where Is Thumbkin?* has children wiggle fingers, touch toes, and act like an elephant. *Wiggle Wiggle* has children shake, jump, and wiggle. (Available from Lakeshore.)

5. At Circle Time. Play "Gotcha!" Tell the children to listen carefully to what each animal says, and if they think the animal is wrong or trying to fool them, say "Gotcha!" Then you pretend to be each of the animals, making a correct sound for all but one: "The dog says ruff-ruff!" "The cat says meow!" "The mouse says squeak-squeak!" "The horse says meow!" Play a variant of this game with sounds of motor vehicles, musical instruments, people walking, or anything else you can think of that makes a special sound. Play a different sound-listening game daily.

SUGGESTED READINGS

Burman, L. (2009). *Are you listening? Fostering conversations that help young children learn.* St. Paul, MN: Redleaf Press.

Jalongo, M. R. (2008). *Learning to listen, listening to learn.* Washington, DC: National Association for the Education of Young Children (NAEYC).

Roskos, K. A., Tabors, P. O., & Lenhart, L. A. (2009). *Oral language and early literacy in preschool: Talking, reading, and writing.* 2nd ed. Newark, DE: International Reading Association.

4 Listening Center

CONCEPT

A listening center is new to many early childhood classrooms. If you are serious about promoting children's listening, you should have a special center like this for special listening and speaking. You might set it up like a TV or radio studio with a pretend microphone or a children's karaoke machine to speak into. A tape or CD player with several headsets can be used for listening to recordings children make of pretend "news reports" or for listening to children's books on tapes or CDs. Be sure to have a book on hand for every book tape or CD you use. Encourage listeners to turn the pages of the books as they hear the words being read. Headphones are important to give each child a personal listening experience of hearing the story, as well as to prevent the recorded story from disturbing other children.

Activities

1. Read-along books. When children are listening to a book, be sure to check to see if the child can really follow along in the book and turn the pages at the right time.

Your listening center can contain headsets and a tape/CD player.

You may want to put on a headset and help a new child learn how to follow along with the CD.

FIGURE 4–1 Scholastic Listening Library.

Boom Chicka Rock	*If You Take a Mouse to the Movies*
Chicka Chicka 1, 2, 3	*Is Your Mama a Llama?*
Chicks and Salsa	*K Is for Kissing a Cool Kangaroo*
Corduroy	*The Little Red Hen*
Duck on a Bike	*The Mitten*
Giggle, Giggle, Quack	*Giraffes Can't Dance*

2. Teacher read-along. You may want to put on a headset yourself and follow along with the story so a child new to the experience understands how it works and what she needs to do. Scholastic (1-800-724-6527) has several "Listening Libraries" with 15 audio CDs each and two copies of each matching title. (See Figure 4–1 for a sample; also in Spanish.)

SUGGESTED READINGS

Beaty, J. J., & Pratt, L. (2011). *Early literacy in preschool and kindergarten: A multicultural perspective.* 3rd ed. Boston: Pearson.
Bullard, J. (2010). *Creating environments for learning.* Columbus, OH: Pearson.

5 Talk-Rich Environment

Conversations

Children in preschool learn the most about words and how they are used through the rich conversations they listen to and participate in with their teachers and peers. Morrison (2004) tells us: "In conversation, adults and children share information in a personal give and take. Conversations may be about feelings, ideas or events in their personal lives. Conversations that are honest and sincere, rather than didactic and contrived, help children build trusting relationships with adults" (p. 27). Roskos, Tabors, and Lenhart (2009) talk about "substantive conversation" that adults use to engage children in long and rich dialogues about important topics (p. 39).

Because oral language is the basis for emergent literacy, teachers need to provide opportunities for rich talk with every child every day. The snack and lunch tables are excellent locations for such informal conversations to occur with the children around you. Keep track daily of which children you talk with, and make it a point to talk the next day with those who were left out. Be sure there are several cell phones (minus their batteries) available for pretend calls to such children. Even shy children who may not respond easily to a teacher face-to-face will do pretend talking on a cell phone. Child-child

Pretend phone calls to a friend on Jupiter promote exciting conversations.

Adding details

Teacher: Hi Cody, I see you are putting a lot of red marks in your journal today. Is it about our trip to the fire station?

Child: Yep. This is a big fire truck.

Teacher: Good. The firefighters didn't wear any red at all, did they?

Child: Their hats were yellow.

Teacher: Yes. They called them "helmets." Do you remember?

Explaining terms

Child: Some of them had tanks on their backs.

Teacher: Yes. They called them a Self-Contained Breathing Apparatus, for breathing oxygen in case a building was full of smoke.

Sharing experiences

Child: I want to be a fireman when I grow up.

Teacher: I have a friend who is a volunteer firefighter. Maybe she will come to our class and talk about her work.

Wonder aloud

Child: Does your friend live at the firehouse?

Teacher: I don't think so. I wonder how she hears the fire alarm.

FIGURE 5–1   Conversation Stretchers.

conversations can take place anywhere in the room, but are especially important during impromptu dramatic play scenarios. (See Strategy 6, "Dramatic Play.")

Teachers can promote longer and richer conversations with children by using conversational strategies such as adding details to the conversation, explaining terms, sharing experiences, or wondering aloud. Figure 5–1 describes how these conversation stretchers might work for a teacher talking with children about the field trip they took to the fire station. Other activities to promote conversations include the following:

Activities

1. Snack Talk. Sit at one of the tables where children are eating their snack. After most of the snack has been eaten, choose one of the children to be the "snack talker" for the day. Let that child choose something interesting to talk about (not the snacks) and begin. Children often choose topics such as their pets, their baby sister, their new trike, or going to Grandma's house. Other children can join in the conversation until everyone at the table has had a turn to talk. Remind them that when one child is talking the others must listen and wait their turn to reply. You can be the model snack talker at first to give children the idea.

2. E.T. Phone Home. Sit in a circle with a small group and two toy phones. Pretend you are an extraterrestrial (E.T.) on Earth, phoning a friend on Jupiter (one of the children in the group) to tell him what strange things you have seen on Earth. "They have boys and girls who move by walking with their feet on the ground! They don't know how to fly like we do!" Then hand your phone to the next child and have her "phone home" from Earth to another child in the group.

3. Read books that feature two children having a conversation. A good choice is Child's books about Charlie and Lola, the older brother who wittily persuades his younger sister to resolve each of her problems in books such as **I Will Never Not Ever Eat a Tomato** (Child, L., 2000, Cambridge, MA: Candlewick Press), **I Am Not Sleepy and I Will Not Go to Bed** (2001), or **I Am Too Absolutely Small for School** (2004). The entire books are conversations between Charlie and Lola with Lola giving preposterous reasons why she can't do something and Charlie overcoming her arguments with his own absurd replies. Get listeners involved taking the two roles and thinking up other wacky advice and retorts.

4. Read **Oliver Has Something to Say!** (Edwards, P., 2002, Montreal: Lobster Press). It's about the little boy who wants to talk and give his own opinion, but whose mother, father, and sister always answer for him. At last at preschool his voice bursts out, and once home, he simply overflows with the pent-up answers he always wanted to give. This is a fine book for story drama (see Strategy 13, "Story Drama"), with the children taking all the parts but coming out with their own opinions.

SUGGESTED READINGS

Birckmayer, J., Kennedy, A., & Stonehouse, A. (2010). Sharing spoken language: Sounds, conversations, and told stories. *Young Children, 65*(1), 34–39.

Kalmar, K. (2008). Let's give children something to talk about! Oral language and preschool literacy. *Young Children, 63*(1), 88–92.

Morrison, K. L. (2004). Positive child/adult interactions: Strategies that support children's healthy development. *Dimensions of Early Learning, 32*(2), 23–28.

Roskos, K. A., Tabors, P. O., & Lenhart, L. A. (2009). *Oral language and early literacy in preschool: Talking, reading, and writing.* 2nd ed. Newark, DE: International Reading Association.

6 Dramatic Play

CONCEPT

Dramatic play in an early childhood program is the spontaneous role-play children engage in as they pretend different real-life scenarios. Such pretend play usually takes place in the dramatic play center, which is often set up with child-size kitchen furniture: sink, stove, refrigerator, cupboards, table, chairs, and all sorts of props. Teachers encourage children to pretend about family life, field trips they have taken, community events that have happened, projects they are pursuing, or stories they have listened to.

At times teachers may set up the center to serve as a supermarket, hospital, doctor's clinic, fast-food restaurant, post office, hairdresser's, shoe store, pet shop, fire station, laundromat, or any one of a number of real-life locations the children are familiar with. Props such as appropriate clothes, shoes, hats, purses, implements, and gear related to the roles they will be playing help children make their spontaneous dramas meaningful.

This kind of pretending is the way children make sense of their world. Whether or not such a center is available, they will pretend about events in their lives anyway: Dad starts a new job; a new baby is brought home; Grandma comes for a visit; they have to go to the doctor's for a shot. Emotional situations are especially common themes in children's pretending. Sometimes a scary television program

Getting ready to give the babies a shot.

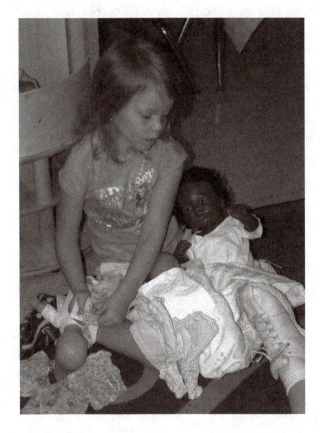

at home prompts a new drama in the classroom. In one classroom, when one child put on a police hat, the other children were uncomfortable at first, but then turned him into a police dog they could control. They built him a high-walled doghouse with the large hollow blocks to contain him. When young children are involved in dramatic play, creative solutions abound.

Where does literacy fit in? Speaking, listening, reading, and writing, the principal elements of literacy, are encouraged and supported more fully by dramatic play than by almost any other early childhood endeavor (see Figure 6–1). Kalmar (2008) points out: "Dramatic play produces a great deal of descriptive language. Children negotiate and develop themes, roles, and rules. Some children like to give directions. 'You're the dad and you take us to school. It's over here.'" (p. 90).

Once children have expressed interest in a particular theme, teachers can stock the dramatic play center with literacy items. Ferguson (1999) describes a restaurant scenario in which preschoolers spontaneously pretended to read, write, and count money. Children read menus, ordered items, wrote orders, read their placemats, and paid for their food.

In every instance the children are obliged to talk to one another. This unprompted child-child conversation is one of the most important contributions of dramatic play to young children's emergent literacy. Children learn to use the words surrounding the theme they are exploring. Those who don't know the appropriate words or how to use them listen to the children who do and soon are imitating them.

Activities

1. *Stimulate talking around dramatic play themes.*
   - Help children experience the topic firsthand through a field trip.
   - Talk with the children afterwards about the field trip.
   - Have children symbolize what they experienced in their drawings, singing, stories.
   - Read children books about the theme.
   - Provide props that will motivate pretend play about the theme.
   - Remain in the background unobtrusively once the play has started.
   - Listen, observe, and take notes on the spontaneous conversations.
   - Analyze the children's conversations to see what needs to happen next.

2. *Take children on a field trip to a medical clinic.* The children in one class visited the registration area, waiting room, examining room, and x-ray room of a doctor's clinic. Over the next few days they talked about what they had seen, painted pictures of it, and made and painted an x-ray machine out of a cardboard carton.

3. *Read appropriate books about the theme.*

   Doctor Ted (Beaty, A., 2008, New York: McElderry Books).

   I'm Really Ever So Not Well (Child, L., 2007, New York: Dial Books).

- Stimulate talking around dramatic play theme.
- Take children on field trip that supports theme.
- Read appropriate books about theme.
- Set up dramatic play center with theme props.
- Observe and record what occurs in center.
- Analyze children's conversations during play.
- Record children's stories on tape.
- Determine how to extend this experience.

FIGURE 6–1   Dramatic Play to Support Speaking and Listening.

This Is a Hospital, Not a Zoo! (Karim, R., 1998, New York: Clarion Books).

Jessica's X-Ray (Zonta, P., 2002, Buffalo: Firefly Books).

How Do Dinosaurs Get Well Soon? (Yolen, J., 2003, New York: Blue Sky Press).

4. Set up a dramatic play center as a medical clinic. After the field trip, all the children wanted pretend x-rays taken of their babies' "broken arms," so the teacher helped them set up a medical clinic with a waiting area, examining table, and an x-ray area. Literacy props such as a sign-in book, telephone, and magazines were put in the waiting area. Doctors' and nurses' paraphernalia were assembled: stethoscopes, thermometers, syringes, bandages, and long-sleeved men's white shirts for lab coats. As many as six children at a time could play in this dramatic play center clinic.

5. Observe and record what occurs in this dramatic play. Conversations blossomed as children had to negotiate for the roles they wanted and then sign in, wait in the waiting area, and visit the doctor to get shots for the babies or have their arms x-rayed by the technician. As children drifted in and out of the play, each group played the scenario somewhat differently. Sometimes one child would take over as the leader and assign roles: "I'll be the x-ray technician. You be the doctor. You others can bring your babies for shots and x-rays."

Everyone wanted to be the x-ray technician. The x-ray technicians in this classroom got to draw pretend x-rays (mostly lines and squiggles) on transparent sheets, and everyone wanted to do it. They had seen real x-rays on their clinic visit, as well as the ones in the book *Jessica's X-Ray*. They were intrigued with the idea of looking at bones inside the body. To make it even more realistic, the teacher brought in a little plastic skeleton from a science store. More negotiations ensued. Finally the leader gave in: "Okay. You can all be x-ray technicians who come to visit my clinic. I'll be the doctor."

6. Analyze the children's conversations during their play. Staff members who listened to the clinic conversations every day recorded the following types of dialogue:

- *Assigning or negotiating roles* (doctor): "You be the x-ray technician today."
- *Directing the action* (x-ray technician): "No. You have to wait for your turn."
- *Sustaining the action* (technician): "Let's go out and get more babies."
- *Expressing feelings* (mother): "Oh, will it hurt? Don't hurt my baby."
- *Giving and receiving feedback* (mothers, fathers): "That's not how you give a shot. You put it in there." "Where is my x-ray?" "That don't look right."
- *Renegotiating roles* (fathers): "It's my turn to be the x-ray man."

7. Record children's stories on tape. So much good conversation was occurring that the teacher invited players to record what happened on their visit to the clinic on a tape cassette. Later it was transcribed into a class book of "Our Visit to the Clinic" for everyone to see and hear.

8. Determine how to extend this experience. Later the teacher and staff in this classroom decided to extend the children's interest in bones with a visit to a science museum to look at dinosaur bones. They already had many picture storybooks on dinosaurs. In related activities, perhaps the children would want to "dig for dinosaur bones" in the sand table, or make model dinosaurs out of clay, or set up a dinosaur museum with their toy dinosaurs in the block center. Signs, labels, drawings, conversations, stories, and songs: all kinds of literacy activities would surely result.

SUGGESTED READINGS

Beaty, J. J., & Pratt, L. (2011). *Early literacy in preschool and kindergarten: A multicultural perspective.* 3rd ed. Boston: Pearson.

Ferguson, C. J. (1999). Building literacy with child-constructed sociodramatic play centers. *Dimensions of Early Childhood, 27*(3), 23–29.

Kalmar, K. (2008). Let's give children something to talk about! Oral language and preschool literacy. *Young Children, 63*(1), 88–92.

Rowe, D. W. (2000). Bringing books to life: The role of book-related dramatic play in young children's literacy learning. In K. A. Roskos & J. F. Christie (Eds.), *Play and literacy in early childhood: Research from multiple perspectives*. Mahwah, NJ: Lawrence Erlbaum.

7  Dual Language Learners

CONCEPT

Young children can acquire a second language naturally without being taught, just as they did their first language: (1) by being immersed in it, (2) by hearing it spoken around them, and (3) by interacting with speakers of the language. Children of preschool age (3, 4, and 5) have brains that are wired to acquire language in this fashion. Thus, when they are immersed in English in the preschool classroom, they pick up a great deal of the language on their own by hearing it spoken and interacting with child speakers their own age.

Cheatham and Ro (2010) tell us, "When children are learning two languages they develop *interlanguage*—a transitory grammar based on rules they have observed in their home language and those they observe in their new language" (p. 19). Some dual language learner (DLL) preschool children remain silent for long periods as they absorb the new language around them. Others pick up a few English words and mix them up with their home language in what is called "code switching." Remember not to correct them. This is a typical progression in learning a second language and no cause for concern. They will straighten out their two languages as they become fluent.

Figure 7–1, "Helping DLL Children Learn English," gives suggestions you may want to use. Helping the children feel welcome and a part of the class is the most important. Try to have at least one bilingual speaker among your adult staff or someone who can translate, especially with parents. Teaching by direct translation should be avoided, however, so that children do not tune out one of the languages in favor of another, according to Stechuk and Burns (2005). On the other hand, you must encourage and accept the language used by individual children, whatever it is. Although children should be involved in conversations with adults who speak both languages, these adults should try not to code switch themselves, but keep to one language at a time.

The dramatic play center is particularly suitable for children's emergence into a second language. As Burton and Edwards (2006) tell us, "A dramatic play center is especially useful for children who are English language learners. Pretend play enables them to communicate in an informal setting and

Some bilingual children spend time playing silently before they attempt to speak English.

- Make children feel welcome.
- Accept children's own language.
- Pronounce children's names correctly.
- Use gestures, body language to communicate.
- Speak slowly, clearly.
- Learn key words in children's language.
- Encourage family involvement.
- Read bilingual books.
- Be patient.

FIGURE 7–1   Helping DLL Children Learn English.

gather information that will be helpful to them, even beyond the classroom" (p. 6). Because children learn more easily in situations they are familiar with, you should set up your center with props from familiar settings: kitchen, restaurant, store, doctor's office.

Activities

1. Children need to know there are many languages all over the world. September 21 has been declared the International Day of Peace by the United Nations. Obtain a copy of the picture book **Can You Say Peace?** (Katz, K., 2006), showing pictures of the faces of 11 children, each saying "peace" in his or her own language. Talk with the children about what peace means for all of us. Scan and laminate the book pictures and have each child in your reading group hold one and say "peace" in that child's language as you read the simple story and come to that page. Afterwards string the pictures up into a wonderful mobile.

2. Read bilingual picture books to the children. A number of favorite children's picture books have been translated into Spanish and published in Spanish alone. For preschool children who are dual language learners, bilingual picture books are more appropriate with both English and the home language featured. They should be read to the children in both languages. If you do not speak Spanish, for instance, ask one of the children's relatives or friends to come in and read the book. Send a copy of the book home for the family to enjoy. Be ready to read it again and again in the classroom in both languages. It is important for all the children to know about a language different from their own. Extension activities should then be planned in learning centers throughout the classroom. Here are several simple bilingual books in English and Spanish easy for the children to follow and understand:

> **Abuelita Full of Life** (Costales, A., 2007, Flagstaff, AZ: Luna Rising).
>
> **Margaret and Margarita** (Reiser, L., 1993, New York: Greenwillow).
>
> **Play Lady** (Hoffman, E., 1999, St. Paul, MN: Redleaf Press).

Here are bilingual books in English and Navajo:

> **Dragonfly Kites** (Highway, T., 2002, New York: HarperCollins).
>
> **Johonaa'ei: Bringer of Dawn** (Tsinajinnie, V., 2007, Flagstaff, AZ: Salina Bookshelf).
>
> **Red Is Beautiful** (John, R., 2003, Flagstaff, AZ: Salina Bookshelf).

3. Read a bilingual cumulative tale. **The Empanadas That Abuela Made** (Bertrand, D. G., 2003, Houston, TX: Pinata Books) is about the pumpkin tarts that Grandma made, as described in Strategy 2, "Speaking Words." On each page a new ingredient is added to the one before. The reader (and the children) must repeat the accumulating ingredients one by one every time a new one is added. It's great fun to do this with everyone chanting first in English, then in Spanish. Everyone will be learning new vocabulary words in both languages before you are finished. But the extension activity is the most fun of all: actually making pumpkin empanadas in the classroom (in both languages)!

4. *Set up the dramatic play center as a supermarket.* Use props of empty food boxes, plastic fruits, shopping bags, carrying baskets, and several boxes of animal crackers. Then read the English picture book ***Bebé Goes Shopping*** (Elya, S. M., 2006, Orlando, FL: Harcourt) about Mama taking Bebé to the supermarket. Every English sentence has a Spanish word (translated in the glossary) about something the mother or baby sees or does. Baby in the shopping cart is looking for a *dulce* (sweet) but grabs what he can off the shelves. He drops her keys, bites her shopping list, but finally she finds him a box of animal crackers, and he spends the rest of the trip biting pieces off the animal crackers. Read the book over and over with the children saying the Spanish words and finally eating real animal crackers.

SUGGESTED READINGS

Burton, S. J., & Edwards, L. C. (2006). Creative play: Building connections with children who are learning English. *Dimensions of Early Childhood, 34*(2), 3–8.

Cheatham, G. A., & Ro, Y. B. (2010). Young English learners' *interlanguage* as a context for language and early literacy development. *Young Children, 65*(4), 18–23.

Konishi, C. (2007). Learning English as a second language: A case study of a Chinese girl in an American preschool. *Childhood Education, 83*(5), 267–272.

Shin, S. J. (2010). Teaching English language learners: Recommendations for early childhood educators. *Dimensions of Early Childhood, 38*(2), 13–20.

Stechuk, R. A., & Burns, M. S. (2005). Does it matter how adults use children's first language and English when they talk to preschoolers? *Young Children, 60*(6), 42–43.

Sundem, G., Krieger, J., & Pikiewicz, K. (2008). 10 languages you'll need most in the classroom. Thousand Oaks, CA: Corwin Press.

8 Phonological Awareness

CONCEPT

Word Play

We know that young children learn through self-discovery play. They manipulate, master, and make meaning of every object in their environment if given the opportunity to play. Is it surprising, then, that young children in the early stages of language development also play with words? They try out word sounds, make up nonsense words, and repeat rhyming words over and over. Most people pay little attention to this activity because it seems so inconsequential. But then we learn that many young children who have been involved in early rhyming activities such as nursery rhymes are often more successful in reading later on.

Why is this? Some research tells us that to fully understand spoken language, young children need to develop *phonological awareness,* that is, an awareness of speech sounds, especially word sounds. Yopp and Yopp (2010) say: "Phonological awareness is sensitivity to the sound structure of language. It demands the ability to turn one's attention to sounds in spoken language while temporarily shifting away from its meaning" (p. 12). Children who can detect and manipulate sounds in speech are phonologically aware.

Part of this awareness is *rhyme recognition,* the hearing and recognizing of words that sound alike, and *alliteration recognition,* the hearing and recognizing of words that start the same. Although it is not known for sure how much phonological awareness is necessary for successful reading, we do know that "children appear to hear rhyming words and words that begin the same first" and that "phonological awareness is related to reading success" (Opitz, 2000, p. 11).

Does this mean we should formally teach children to recognize rhymes? No. Just as children learn to write mainly through discovery, for the majority of children phonological awareness is more caught than taught (Opitz, 2000, p. 13). It is "caught" in homes where mothers and fathers say nursery rhymes and play pat-a-cake games with their little ones and in homes where children themselves carry on monologues in which they manipulate sounds, patterns, and meanings of words as they try to understand the language they hear.

Have the children repeat the words that sound alike.

FIGURE 8–1 Books Featuring Rhyming.

> *Grumpy Gloria*
>
> *"Fire, Fire!" Said Mrs. McGuire*
>
> *Is Your Mama a Llama?*
>
> *Llama Llama Misses Mama*
>
> *Do You Do a Didgeridoo?*
>
> *Guinea Pigs Add Up*
>
> *I'm Your Bus*

Schwartz (1981) found that infants from 6 to 18 months often talk or sing themselves to sleep repeating rhythmic and rhyming word-sounds. On the other hand, preschool youngsters play with real words, sometimes repeating them just under their breath in nonsensical fashion: "Ham-bam-lam-sam-wham-wham-wham." Listen and you may hear some. It is "caught" in early childhood programs that feature singing, chanting, fingerplays, nursery rhymes, predictable stories, word games, and all the other informal language activities described in this text. One of the best ways to foster this word-sound awareness is by reading aloud picture books that focus on specific language elements such as rhyming and alliteration, some of which are shown in Figures 8–1 and 8–2.

Activities

Rhyming

Choose any of these books and read it to one small group at a time. The "trick words" you will be focusing on are the rhyming words. Once the children are familiar with the book after several readings, you can proceed with the rhyming activities. These activities can be used with any rhyming book. You can create other similar games with the children.

1. Discover the rhyming words in **Grumpy Gloria** (Dewdney, A., 2006, New York: Viking).

Word Detectives

Children can become Word Detectives if they can detect the rhyming words in this story. Have the children cover their eyes as you read two pages and listen for the words that sound alike. As in many rhyming books, they are the last word in each sentence. Here are fun rhyming words from *Grumpy Gloria:*

grumpy-lumpy	pout-out	slumpy-grumpy	hair-everywhere
scowl-foul	dog-jog	dumpy-grumpy	dirty-squirty
soapy-mopey	toy-enjoy	jabby-crabby	game-name
ride-inside	shout-out	grouchy-ouchy	who-two

Have the children listen carefully and help them at first so they know what to listen for. Stick a peel-off star onto every listener who names a pair of rhymes. By the end of the book, be sure that everyone is a Word Detective.

2. Discover the rhyming words in **"Fire! Fire!" Said Mrs. McGuire** (Martin, B., 2006, Orlando: Harcourt).

Firefighters

Children can become Firefighters if they find all the rhyming words in this simple, stirring story.

fire-McGuire	floor-Moore	help-Kelp	way-Lei	declare-Wear
where-Bear	top-Kopp	come-Plumb	see-Chi	save us-McDavis
town-Brown	pity-Kitty	water-Votter	door-Orr	potatoes-McDavis

FIGURE 8–2 Books
Featuring Alliteration.

> *Bats at the Beach*
>
> *Cha-Cha Chimps*
>
> *Flip Flop Bop*
>
> *Grumpy Gloria*
>
> *Eleanor, Ellatony, Ellencake, and Me*
>
> *K Is for Kissing a Cool Kangaroo*
>
> *Mammoths on the Move*
>
> *Alligator Arrived with Apples*

Alliteration

Alliteration is different from rhyming. Try not to confuse the two when presenting these concepts to the children. It is better to read books and do activities involving alliteration at a different time from those involving rhyming. Children will be listening for words that start with the same sound. Have them close their eyes and listen to the title of each of these very different books that feature alliteration (see Figure 8–2) before you read the story. Can they hear the words that start with the same sound?

*1. Discover the words that start with the same letter sound as in the book **Alligator Arrived with Apples: A Potluck Alphabet Feast*** (Dragonwagon, 1986, New York: Macmillan).

Letter Leader

Children can become Letter Leaders if they can detect all the words that start with the same letter sound on one page in this book. Here are some:

    b: bear, brought, banana bread, biscuits, butter

    c: cat, came, cranberry compote, cherry cobbler

    d: dragon, deer, diced, dates, delivered, door

Give every child who detects one set of these words its plastic letter to hold. Help every child in the small group to receive a letter.

*2. Discover the words that start with the same letter sound in the book **Mammoths on the Move*** (Wheeler, L., 2006, Orlando: Harcourt).

Mammoth Mover

Children can become Mammoth Movers if they can detect all the words that start with the same sound on a page. This may be more difficult as the book is full of rhyming words that don't show alliteration. Have children listen closely for beginning word sounds on every page, such as:

    comfy-coats; snarly-snaggy; wonderful-woolly; two-toothy-tusks; chewing-chawing;

    wise-woolly; stepping-stomping; watch-woolly; way-woolly; tramping-trembling;

    wary-woolly; danger-danger-danger; big-bulky; huge-hulky; wide-woolly; crashing-clashing;

    trekking-trudging-treading; willful-woolly; week-week; day-day; wonderful-woolly.

After reading the story to a small group, have the Mammoth Movers (everyone) move in a single-file line around the room, swinging their trunks (arms), and moving like mammoths as you read the story again. Do they want to do it again? When children have fun with word sounds they will want to repeat the activity over and over.

SUGGESTED READINGS

Hohman, M. (2002). *Fee, fi, phonemic awareness: 130 prereading activities for preschoolers.* Ypsilanti, MI: High Scope Press.

Opitz, M. F. (2000). *Rhymes & reasons: Literature and language play for phonological awareness.* Portsmouth, NH: Heinemann.

Sanacore, J. (2010). Connecting rimes to meaningful contexts. *Childhood Education, 86*(4), 241–248.

Schwartz, J. I. (1981). Children's experiments with language. *Young Children, 36*(5), 16–26.

Yopp, H. K., & Yopp, R. H. (2009). Phonological awareness is child's play! *Young Children, 64*(1), 12–18.

9 Chanting/Singing

CONCEPT 1

Chanting

Chanting is "any group of words that is recited together with a lively beat" (Buchoff, 1994). When young children speak in unison as they do in chanting, they learn the importance of clear and expressive pronunciation of words. Chanting involves rhyming words and repetition, as well as a catchy rhythm that takes hold of the listener and won't let go. Most advertising jingles, cheers at sporting events, and jump-rope rhymes are forms of chanting everyone recognizes.

Because children love to recite chants over and over, they learn to say unfamiliar words just for the effect they produce when they rhyme. The rhythm and the rhyming help them to remember the words and the chant itself. Chants help pave the language circuits in the brain for using new words the children will eventually learn to read. Even children who speak nonstandard English and those who are learning English as a second language love to chant, and their copying of what the group is chanting helps them learn the standard language.

This boy sings through a karaoke machine.

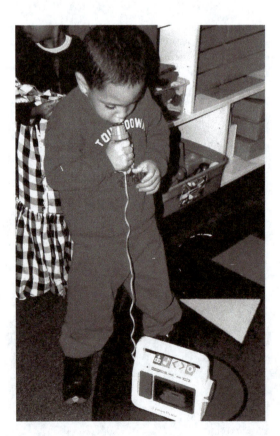

Activities 1

Many teachers look for chants in the picture books they will be reading to the children.

1. Read **The Lady with the Alligator Purse** (Westcott, N., 1988, Boston: Little, Brown). This story revolves around the traditional jump-rope rhyme whose verses end with the same catchy phrase:

> Call for the doctor,
>
> Call for the nurse,
>
> Call for the lady with the alligator purse.

In this book Tiny Tim swallows the bathtub water and soap, but when the doctor calls for penicillin and the nurse calls for castor oil, the lady opens her alligator purse and out pops pizza. So be ready to have a pizza party. Afterwards, have children make up their own stories about different characters and what happens when the doctor comes. Can they do them as chants?

2. Read **Dinosaurumpus** (Mitton, T., 2002, New York: Orchard Books). Children's attraction to dinosaurs will certainly be satisfied with this book since it is all in rhymes that make fine chants. A new dinosaur enters on every page, demonstrating his steps. Children can join in the chant at the end of each page and later become the dancing dinosaurs themselves.

3. Read **Miss Mary Mack** (Hoberman, M. A., 1998, Boston: Little, Brown). Here is another classic chant children love to recite. In this case, Miss Mary Mack, Mack, Mack, all dressed in black, black, black ends up jumping the fence for 50 cents every day with the elephant. It is important for you to follow up children's favorite chants like this with some of your own. Chants can be used to tell time, give messages, or give directions children follow with glee. For example:

> Pick up the blocks, blocks, blocks;
>
> Don't watch the clocks, clocks, clocks.
>
> Put all the books, books, books
>
> Back in their nooks, nooks, nooks.
>
> Put on your jacket, jacket, jacket;
>
> Don't make a racket, racket, racket.
>
> Walk down the hall, hall, hall;
>
> And that is all, all, all.

Physical Movements to Chants

Wait until children have learned the chants by heart before you add physical responses. Soon they will all want to clap as they call out the chant. Clapping to a beat is an important rhythmical accomplishment that not every preschool child learns immediately. Have them practice by clapping out each child's name according to the syllables.

Once children can clap to simple chants, have them march around the room saying the chant and clapping at the same time. Some picture books show people moving or dancing to the beat of a chant. After they know the chants they can foot-stamp or toe-tap while seated, when standing, or while moving along.

4. Read **Rap a Tap Tap: Here's Bojangles—Think of That!** (Dillon, L., & Dillon, D., 2002, New York: Blue Sky Press). In colorful silhouette-like cutouts, Bojangles taps through every double page of this book as he joyfully dances his way across city streets in rhyming verse. The one-sentence text at the bottom of every left-hand page is followed by the chant. Soon children should be able to rap-a-tap-tap around the room in a follow-the-leader line as you read the book.

5. Read **Twist with a Burger, Jitter with a Bug** (Lowery, L., 1995, Boston: Houghton Mifflin). Another book children can't seem to leave alone is this wonderful jig-sway-polka-twist story in which colorful multiethnic cartoon characters "dance to a mambo, snap to a rap, put on their cleats and tap, tap, tap." Children love to "rattle in their bones up a dark, dark street" in hats of every description, with walking sticks, and wearing colored scarves. The whole group can call out the chant while one or two children demonstrate the actions; or all the children can form a conga line around the room with everyone chanting and dancing.

Buchoff (1994) advises: "Give children opportunities to experiment with the rhythm and tempo of the chant, and encourage them to try different actions. By varying the response, children have the opportunity to recite the same chant multiple times but with novel approaches" (p. 29).

CONCEPT 2

Singing

Singing and speaking have similar roots. They both evolve from the early vocalizations of infants and young children. Most children learn to speak by hearing language spoken around them. They could just as easily learn to sing by hearing songs sung around them. This is certainly the case among many non-Western and indigenous people who make singing a natural part of their life. If the children in your class are not used to singing, you can introduce them to this special skill that can be just as important in learning to read as speaking is.

Singing helps children to develop the rhythmic patterns of language and to recognize the sounds of rhyming words just as chanting does. It taps into the right hemisphere of the brain, which operates both the music and memory functions. It connects the right hemisphere with the left hemisphere, which operates speaking and reading. The steady beat of singing develops pathways in the brain that appear to be essential for learning, especially as related to reading (Snyder, 1997, pp. 169–170).

Singing is a natural language for young children that speaks to them in tones they can relate to. Sing a song in the classroom and you quickly have everyone's attention. Waltz around the room as you sing and the children will soon be up on their feet following you. Children perk up and listen when you sing a musical transition or give directions in song. Are you having trouble getting children to pick up the blocks? Sing them a challenge like this to the tune of "Here We Go round the Mulberry Bush":

> Who can pick the blocks up now,
>
> Blocks up now, blocks up now?
>
> Who can pick the blocks up now,
>
> Before I finish singing? (repeat)

Why do songs seem to work better than words? Perhaps it is the melodic tones that children respond to, making things sound like fun rather than a chore. Maybe it is the rhythm that resonates with children's own heartbeat. Whatever the reason, teachers of young children know that music makes a difference in the classroom. Snyder (1997) also says, "There is evidence that music is pre-literate, emerging before word language, and actually encompassing word language through common expressive features of pitch, duration, stress, tone, color, dynamics, tempo, and phrase, and sometimes use of words" (p. 166).

For music to be meaningful, there must be active involvement by the children in which they take part in the singing while interacting with others. Hands-on, direct musical experiences are best, because they allow children to listen to, engage in, and learn from the singing. Neely (2001) suggests that adults and children can engage in *musical conversations* "in which children make learning connections through their music making" (p. 35).

Activities 2

1. What if you are not a singer? What if you are not a singer and can't carry a tune? Try it anyway. It's important for the children. Start with a monotone. Sing (don't say):

> Rain, <u>rain,</u> go a-<u>way,</u>
>
> Come a-<u>gain</u> another <u>day;</u>
>
> All the <u>children</u> want to <u>play.</u>

Alphabet Song	Jack and Jill
Are You Sleeping?	John Jacob Jingleheimer Schmidt
Do the Hokey Pokey	London Bridge Is Falling Down
Down by the Station	Mary Had a Little Lamb
Eensy Weensy Spider	Ring around the Rosy
Go in and out the Windows	Row, Row, Row Your Boat
Here We Go Looby Loo	Shoo Fly
Here We Go round the Mulberry Bush	Three Blind Mice
Hickory Dickory Dock	Twinkle, Twinkle Little Star
If You're Happy and You Know It	Wheels on the Bus

FIGURE 9–1   Traditional Nursery Songs.

Now drop down a tone when you come to the underlined words. Sing it; don't say it. There! You are singing! Take home recordings of children's traditional nursery songs and play them over and over. Try singing along with them. Choose the ones that are easiest for you to use with the children. Some traditional titles are shown in Figure 9–1.

2. Make "musical conversations" from old songs with new words. Now that you have a repertoire of familiar songs to sing with the children (even two is a repertoire!), you can begin your musical conversations. First sing the song with the children over and over using the traditional words until you know they are familiar with the tune. Now you can use that tune for your musical conversations. What will you talk about? What about feelings, hunger, waiting, weather, sleepiness, listening, congratulations, and special occasions?

One teacher chose to use the tune for "Here We Go round the Mulberry Bush" every time the class got ready to go outside. They soon came to recognize the tune as a signal to get ready. Sometimes the teacher would hum the tune or whistle it. They even recognized the get-ready signal when the teacher tapped it on a drum without saying a word. She used different words whenever the occasion called for them.

> Now it's time to go outside, go outside, go outside;
>
> Now it's time to go outside;
>
> Everyone get ready.
>
> *or*
>
> Allison and Kyle are ready now, ready now, ready now;
>
> Yolanda and Keshawn are ready now;
>
> Everyone else is not!

SUGGESTED READINGS

Beaty, J. J., & Pratt, L. (2011). *Early literacy in preschool and kindergarten: A multicultural perspective.* 3rd ed. Boston: Pearson.

Buchoff, R. (1994). Joyful voices: Facilitating language growth through the rhythmic response to chants. *Young Children, 49*(4), 26–30.

Neely, L. P. (2001). Developmentally appropriate music practice: Children learn what they live. *Young Children, 56*(3), 32–37.

Palmer, H. (2001). The music, movement, and learning connection. *Young Children, 56*(5), 13–17.

Snyder, S. (1997). Developing musical intelligence: Why & how. *Early Childhood Education Journal, 24*(3), 165–171.

10 Vocabulary Development

CONCEPT

Early literacy for young children is based on words. At first the words are spoken by the adults around them. Soon children come to understand what these words mean. Then they learn to speak the words themselves. Eventually they come to write these words and to read what they have written. These words are part of what we call their *vocabulary*. Roskos, Tabors, and Lenhart (2009) tell us: "From age 3 onward they should build a vocabulary of at least 2,500 words per year. They should encounter and explore at least two to four new words each day" (p. 1). Some children come to school with far fewer words than others. For instance, some 3-year-old children from low-income families know 600 fewer words than children the same age from upper-income families. By Grade 2 the gap widens to 4,000 words (Christ & Wang, 2010).

How is it in your classroom? Without a doubt many different words are spoken by you and your team on a daily basis. But do the children realize which ones are new words? Do they understand what these words mean? Can they use any of these new words themselves? Adults who use complex words among themselves need to simplify their language when speaking to children. Don't make it too simple.

It is important to remember that young children learn new words by hearing them spoken and seeing them demonstrated. Children need to recognize these *word-meaning clues*. In the book **Gumption**

Some children made silly animals from rolled Play-Doh.

(Broach, E., 2010), Uncle Nigel, an explorer in Africa, takes his young nephew Peter on a hike into the jungle, explaining that he will need hiking shorts, a canteen, and a lot of "gumption." What is gumption? Peter wonders. Uncle Nigel does not explain that gumption means "courage, spunk, and resourcefulness." Instead, each time Peter says he can't go any farther, Uncle Nigel replies: "Nonsense, my boy. All it takes is a little gumption," and proceeds to demonstrate by hacking his way through the prickly leaves with his hunting knife, or by plunging across a crocodile-infested stream in his life jacket, or by using his rope to climb a mountain. Can your listeners use these pictures as *word-meaning clues* to figure out what "gumption" means? After you read this story, listen to see if any of the children use the word "gumption" in the classroom. If not, maybe they need to hear the story again. Maybe you also need to use the word in classroom conversations.

Help your children to become "word explorers." Although they may pick up many new words if they are spoken over and over, children will learn many more in the activities you provide such as reading aloud, word play, and dramatic play—especially if you point out the new words and write them down. For instance, choose the books you read for their interesting and unusual words. These words can then be featured in the daily activities the children enjoy.

Activities

1. Read **Tony Baloney** *(Ryan, P. M., 2011).* Tony Baloney is a macaroni penguin, a boy penguin in the middle of a large family of girl penguins. He stays away from the baby Baloneys because they are so *exasperating*. If your children are listening for new words, *exasperating* will surely be one. What does it mean? Do the children guess that it means "annoying" or "upsetting"? Then Tony's animal pet Dandelion *runs amok* among the babies' toys. The illustrations show him running "out-of-control." Finally Tony and Dandelion decide they both have to *apologize* (say they're sorry) for their bad behavior. Read the story again and have your listeners substitute a familiar word for the new words. Read the story as many times as the children want to hear it—and you may be hearing children use their new words in other classroom situations. Write each new word on a card and pull out the card from time to time to see if the children still remember the word and can demonstrate its meaning.

2. Read **Looking for a Moose** *(Root, 2006, Cambridge, MA: Candlewick Press).* Four little cartoon children go into the woods looking for a moose—a long-leggy, branchy-antler, dinner-diving, bulgy-nose moose. Have a small group of listeners sit close to see if they can see the moose on any page. Do your listeners know what a moose looks like? Then they may be just like the children in the story. Only parts of this huge animal are visible on each page until the end. Does anyone see them? The new words may be just as confusing as the pictures. What is an antler—a branchy antler? What is a bulgy-nose? Read the book more than once to see if the children can find and name the visible part

FIGURE 10–1 One child called her animal a "leggy-neck leaf-gobbler."

Dakota

of the hiding moose. Other comical new word combinations should also attract their attention: *tilty-stilty, wobbly-knobbly* woods.

3. Have children create their own wacky animals with new word names. Some children may want to make silly animals from rolled Play-Doh. Some can get plastic zoo animals from the block center and paste funny new legs, tails, and even wings on them. One girl drew her wacky animal in the art center, calling it a *leggy-neck leaf-gobbler* (see Figure 10–1). Everyone wanted the animal names on cards. Can the children "read" (remember) the names on the cards? Hold up each card another day and see who can match it with its animal.

SUGGESTED READINGS

Beaty, J. J., & Pratt, L. (2011). *Early literacy in preschool and kindergarten: A multicultural perspective.* 3rd ed. Boston: Pearson.

Christ, T., & Wang, X. C. (2010). Bridging the vocabulary gap: What research tells us about vocabulary instruction in early childhood. *Young Children, 65*(4), 84–91.

Roskos, K. A., Tabors, P. O., & Lenhart, L. A. (2009). *Oral language and early literacy in preschool: Talking, reading, and writing.* 2nd ed. Newark, DE: International Reading Association.

Yopp, H. K., & Yopp, R. H. (2009). Phonological awareness is child's play! *Young Children, 64*(1), 12–18.

11 Book Read-Alouds

CONCEPT

Everyone knows children love to have stories read to them. Early childhood teachers have long included story reading as an important part of their programs. Research has finally determined that this activity is indeed essential in children's development of literacy. The National Association for the Education of Young Children (1998) states: "The single most important activity for building these understandings and skills essential for reading success appears to be reading aloud to children" (p. 33).

We now know why an adult's reading aloud of stories specifically helps children learn to read by themselves. Neuroscientists have discovered that learning to read relies on brain circuits already in place for language. This means that children must use these language circuits before circuits for reading can be established. Reading stories aloud uses language circuits. Hearing stories read aloud helps children develop these circuits in the following ways:

- Children hear the sounds of the words from a book spoken aloud.
- They come to recognize these words by their sounds.
- They come to learn the meaning of these words by the book pictures that illustrate the words, as well as by the story action.
- Eventually they come to learn that these words are also represented in the book by print that they can point out.
- They come to love these books and are motivated to learn to read.

We have also learned that when children hear stories, their brains make images in their minds. These visual images promote memory development. The more frequently they hear favorite stories, the more they remember about them. Often children may correct a reader if she leaves out even one word during her rereading of a favorite book. Eventually some children are able to "read" (tell) an entire story almost verbatim from memory alone. This is one way "reading circuits" are established in the brain.

Reading books to a small group brings them closer to the characters.

FIGURE 11–1   Good Books
for Reading Aloud.

Alligator Baby, Munsch, R., 1997

Bats at the Beach, Lies, B., 2006

Bee-Bim Bop! Park, L., 2005

Captain Cheech, Marin, C., 2008

Drat That Fat Cat! Thompson, P., 2003

Fire! Fire! Said Mrs. McGuire, Martin, B., 2006

Friday My Radio Flyer Flew, Pullen, Z., 2008

Grumpy Gloria, Dewdney, A., 2006

I Love Bugs! Dodd, E., 2010

I'm Your Bus, Singer, M., 2009

Llama Llama Misses Mama, Dewdney, A., 2009

But there is even more to be gained than that. Sipe (2008) tells us: "When we read picture storybooks to children in the early years of school, we are doing much more than simply indoctrinating them into the world of school-based literacy. We are opening them to the richness, beauty, and fascination of subtle and fascinating stories and gorgeous visual art. We are expanding their aesthetic experience exponentially" (6).

Activities

Books that are simple, colorful, and full of exciting-sounding words are especially important to read over and over to children. Words that rhyme and words that are repeated also help children's memory development. The books listed in Figure 11–1 are among the many that contain rhyming or repeated words. They are available from libraries, the publishers, and educational supply companies.

Reading to Children

Before Reading

1. Read book to yourself. First, you must read the book yourself, looking at the cover picture and deciding how to introduce the story, then looking for interesting words or phrases to emphasize ("word tricks"), and finally deciding how to get the children involved in the story the second time through.

2. Read book aloud to yourself. Once you have made your determinations, you will need to read the book aloud ahead of time to see how it goes and how it sounds. If you wait to read it aloud until you are with the children, you may stumble over words and forget to play your word tricks.

3. Note scary incidents. For example, if you plan to start with the book ***Snip Snap! What's That?*** (Bergman, M., 2005, New York: Greenwillow), you see three frightened-looking children on the cover, running away from something. The top of a large green head with huge eyes stares at the reader from the bottom of the cover. As you read through the book you see a green alligator creeping toward three huddled children. The text asks the same question five times as the alligator comes closer and closer ("Were the children scared?"), and answers it in larger and larger words ("YOU BET THEY WERE!"). Finally, the reader comes to a double-spread page showing nothing but the gator's huge jaws ready to eat the children. Upon turning the page, the action suddenly stops and the children turn on the alligator. They've had enough of all this scary alligator stuff. All together they shout: "ALLIGATOR, YOU GET OUT!" And was the alligator scared? ("YOU BET IT WAS!")

During Reading

1. Introduce book to small group. You may decide to introduce the book to a small group or even two children at a time who will sit as close as possible in order to see the pictures and to participate.

You begin by showing them the book cover, saying the title, **Snip Snap! What's That?** and asking them to look at the cover to decide what they think the book will be about. Then read the book slowly all the way through, playing your "word tricks" but with no child participation during this first reading.

2. Play your word tricks. Your word tricks can consist of moving the book in jerks toward the listeners when the words say: *creeping, creeping, creeping;* shaking the book when the words say: *cried, and cried, and cried;* bouncing the book up and down when the words say: *snip, snap, snip, snap;* sliding the book when the words say: *slithered . . . slithered . . . slithered;* opening the book wider and wider when the words say: *creak, creak, creak;* and moving the book closer when the words say: *closer . . . and closer . . . and closer.*

3. Have the children join in. Every time the book children answer the question "Were the children scared?" have the children in your class say loudly together, "YOU BET THEY WERE!" Also have them say, "ALLIGATOR, YOU GET OUT!" and "YOU BET IT WAS!" at the appropriate times.

4. Use other word tricks. Instead of moving the book you can move your hands differently for the words *creeping, slithered, creak,* and *closer.* For the question "Were the children scared?" you can make it sound scary, or very low, or very high, and or whispery every time you ask it.

After Reading

1. Ask simple questions. Ask a few simple questions after the first reading to get the children thinking about the story and repeating a few of its words. Which character did they like best? Marissa? Eva? Jonathan? The alligator? Why? ("Character" may be a new word for them.) How did the alligator get into the building? Could this story really happen?

Talking about stories after reading them is just as important as the story itself, research tells us. Talking about the characters helps to make them real. Talking about the story also helps children to understand the words they are hearing.

2. Use book as lead-in to activities. Use the book as a lead-in to other classroom activities. For instance, after hearing **Snip Snap! What's That?** some children may want to do easel painting in green of the alligator. Others may want to play with cut-out paper characters (see Strategy 43, "Book Characters") or put on a story drama about the book (see Strategy 13, "Story Drama"). Be sure to put the book out for the children to look at in whatever center they are using at the time. **Snip Snap! What's That?** may seem scary to adults, but it is a fun book for children to scare themselves with—which they love to do. Make it fun for your children by following the sequence shown in Figure 11–2.

---

1. Choose simple, colorful books with exciting-sounding words.
2. Read the book yourself, silently and then aloud.
3. Introduce the book by showing the cover.
4. Read to individuals or small groups, showing the pictures.
5. Use "word tricks" by making actions or sounds for words.
6. Have children participate by saying words or making motions.
7. Ask children what they liked about the characters or story.
8. Use book as a lead-in to other classroom activities.
9. Read the book again and again, and involve the children.

FIGURE 11–2 How to Read Books to Young Children.

SUGGESTED READINGS

Fox, M. (2001). *Why reading aloud to children will change their lives forever.* Portsmouth, NH: Heinemann.

Galda, L., & Cullinan, B. (2000). Reading aloud from culturally diverse literature. In D. C. Strickland & L. M. Morrow (Eds.), *Beginning reading and writing* (pp. 134–142). New York: Teachers College Press.

McVicker, C. J. (2007). Young readers respond: The importance of child participation in emerging literacy. *Young Children, 62*(3), 18–22.

National Association for the Education of Young Children. (1998). Learning to read and write: Developmentally appropriate practices for all classrooms. *Young Children, 53*(4), 30–46.

Sipe, L. R. (2008). *Storytime: Young children's literacy understanding in the classroom.* New York: Teachers College Press.

12

Storytelling

CONCEPT

Oral storytelling is not heard in early childhood classrooms as often as story reading—or as often as it should be. Yet storytelling is one of the most valuable instructional approaches for developing children's oral language comprehension, according to Roskos, Tabors, and Lenhart (2009). It requires children to listen with intent to figure out new words and to use their memories to follow the action of the tale.

Storytelling differs from story read-alouds in several significant ways. The story being told comes from the teller rather than from the words in a book. The story depends on the teller's use of words and gestures rather than on the text and illustrations of a picture book. Furthermore, the teller concentrates on the audience rather than on a book. Both forms of story presentation are important for young children's early literacy learning. But why would teachers want to go through the process of learning to tell a story when all they need to do is pick up a picture book and read it aloud? Because they realize that storytelling has its own advantages:

- Storytelling frees the teller to engage children's attention by being more animated.
- It makes the teller more aware of children's reactions to the story.
- Teller can project more of herself into the story (gestures, expression).
- Teller can tailor the story to children's attention span.
- Teller can elicit individual and group participation more easily.
- Telling can stimulate children to make their own mental images, rather than relying on book illustrations.
- Adult telling can serve as a model for children to emulate in their own storytelling.
- Telling can become the vehicle for emergent readers to present stories.
- Children love it!

The teller can get the group to participate as the story is told.

Picture Book Storytelling

Because this text is focused on bringing young children together with books, the storytelling discussed here will come from stories in appropriate picture books in the classroom. (See Figure 12–1.) These books should be the ones with the following characteristics:

1. PLOT: plot incidents that happen in an easily remembered order.
2. CHARACTERS: one or two interesting characters who speak.
3. REPETITION: words, phrases, or incidents that are repeated.

You will not be using the book itself in your storytelling, so choose books that you love that are not too long or complicated and can easily be remembered. Books with folktale-like plots where three things happen in a certain order are a good choice. But any book you really like can be adapted to this sort of formula for telling. You can use the actual words from the book (especially repeated words) or tell the story in your own words. Some of the books you might choose include those in Figure 12–1.

Activities

*1. Tell the story from **Drat That Fat Cat*** (Thompson, P., 2003, New York: Arthur A. Levine Books). Here is a story children really enjoy—not about the lady who swallows a fly, but about the cat who swallows a lady! You will be telling the story before you show the book to the children. But first you need to prepare in the following manner:

1. Read the book to yourself several times aloud.
2. Outline the story on a file card telling the main incidents and dialogue.
   a. Cat meets a rat and eats him ("squeak, squeak, squeak").
   b. Cat meets a duck and eats him ("quack, quack, quack").
   c. Cat meets a dog and eats him ("woof, woof, woof").
   d. Cat meets an old lady and eats her ("Drat that fat cat!").
   e. Cat swallows a bee whole (the bee stings him: "Oow!").
   f. Cat goes "Hic!" five times; one at a time, out pop bee, rat, duck, dog, and lady.
3. Repeated words: "But was that cat fat enough? NO, HE WAS NOT! So he padded along the path in search of food."

Put the book away and practice telling the story aloud privately. Then tell it to the whole class. Start with the first line of the book and go on from there. ("Once there was a cat, a fat, fat cat.") Use different voice tones for the sounds of the animals inside the cat. Have the children answer in unison, "NO, HE WAS NOT!" each time you ask the question, "But was that cat fat enough?" Be sure to use gestures of eating, swallowing, and slapping at the bee. Children will love it. They will want you to do it again. And then imagine their delight when you show them the book. Put it in the book center and let them investigate it on their own. This story can easily be adapted to any group of animals (jungle animals, dinosaurs, farm animals).

Grumpy Gloria	*Looking for a Moose*
Juan Bobo Goes to Work	*Owl Babies*
Drat That Fat Cat	*Stuck in the Mud*
Alligator Baby	*Giraffes Can't Dance*
Snip Snap! What's That?	*Bebé Goes Shopping*

FIGURE 12–1   Picture Books for Storytelling.

*2. Tell the story from **Owl Babies*** (Waddell, M., 1992, Cambridge, MA: Candlewick Press). Here is another story children love, one about three white baby barn owls (Sarah, Percy, and Bill) in their tree hole at night waiting nervously for the mother owl to return. Outline the story as previously and practice it before you tell it to the class or show them the book. Be sure to use gestures, expression, and animation as you tell the tale.

1. Read the book to yourself several times aloud.
2. Outline the story on a file card telling the main incidents and dialogue.
   a. Sarah thinks she's gone hunting; Percy, to get them food.
   b. Bill always says: I want my mommy! (IWMM).
   c. Owls come out of nest and sit on separate tree branches.
   d. Sarah thinks she'll be back; Percy hopes: back soon; Bill: IWMM!
   e. Sarah thinks she'll bring them mice; Percy supposes so; Bill: IWMM!
   f. Sarah thinks they should all sit on her branch.
   g. Sarah wonders whether she got lost; Percy: or a fox got her; Bill: IWMM!
   h. Close eyes and wish mother would come.
   i. She comes.
   j. Owls flap and dance.
   k. Mother asks why all the fuss; you knew I'd come back.
   l. Sarah knew it; Percy knew it! Bill: I loveMM!
3. Repeated words: "I want my mommy!"

After you have told the story several times have children speak for the owl babies when you come to their parts. Everyone can say Bill's words in unison. Then show the children the book and leave it in the book center for the children to look at. They'll love the large, white owls against the black pages.

3. Encourage children to retell this story or any story they know. As Isbell (2002) notes, for children, the process of telling a story helps them understand how the story works, what phrases are repeated, and what the sequence of action is. Every time they retell a story, they build on their knowledge of what goes into a story and how to make it exciting with their voice and gestures. Do not push children to tell stories or try to tell them perfectly. Accept whatever they do. Storytelling should be fun and exciting for everyone involved.

Children often like to hold the book while they tell the story. They can retell their stories to a small group or even to a partner. The total class is often too overpowering for beginning storytellers. Some will prefer to tell their stories to a tape recorder and listen to them later.

Tape record any of the stories children retell to the group if they agree. They can be transcribed and written into a personal book for the child, or played later for others to enjoy.

SUGGESTED READINGS

Birckmayer, J., Kennedy, A., & Stonehouse, A. (2010). Sharing spoken language: Sounds, conversations, and told stories. *Young Children, 65*(1), 34–39.

Meier, D. R. (Ed.). (2009). *Here's the story: Using narrative to promote young children's language and literacy learning.* New York: Teachers College Press.

Isbell, R. T. (2002). Telling and retelling stories: Learning language and literacy. *Young Children, 57*(2), 26–30.

Roskos, K. A., Tabors, P. O., & Lenhart, L. A. (2009). *Oral language and early literacy in preschool: Talking, reading, and writing.* 2nd ed. Newark, DE: International Reading Association.

Sipe, L. R. (2008). *Storytime: Young children's literary understanding in the classroom.* New York: Teachers College Press.

13 Story Drama

CONCEPT

One of the best ways to make picture books memorable for children is through story drama— sometimes called "story reenactments." They are informal, on-the-spot dramas performed by the children about a familiar story while you are reading it. The drama is for the children themselves and not an audience—unless the children want one. They can be simple stories having only a few characters, like **Owl Babies** (Waddell, M., 1992, Cambridge, MA: Candlewick Press) with its three baby owls and the mother. (See Strategy 12, "Storytelling.") Or they can be quite complex, like **Giraffes Can't Dance** (Andrae, G., 2001, New York: Orchard Books) with a whole collection of jungle animals.

Books best suited for story reenactments are those with several characters who talk, with a lot of action, and with a minimum of text. Rhyming and predictable books are best because they help children memorize the words. It is not necessary for children to repeat all the dialogue in the text, for you will be reading it as they act it out. But most children want to say a few words or at least make animal sounds. Costumes also are not necessary, but again, children like to wear hats, animal ears they have made, or at least a sign around their necks telling who they are.

Some books well suited to story reenactments are found in Figure 13–1. If children want to reenact more complex stories, you can adapt them. Pretending is serious business for young children, and to be able to pretend about the story in a book gives them great satisfaction.

Getting dressed as Elizabeth Blackwell in My Name Is Not Isabella.

Drat That Fat Cat, Thompson, P., 2003

Giraffes Can't Dance, Andreae, G., 2001

Grumpy Gloria, Dewdney, A., 2006

Looking for a Moose, Root, P., 2006

My Name Is Not Alexander, Fosberry, J., 2011

My Name Is Not Isabella, Fosberry, J., 2010

Owl Babies, Waddell, M., 1992

Sometimes I'm Bombaloo, Vail, R., 2002

Snip Snap! What's That? Bergman, M., 2005

Stuck in the Mud, Clarke, J., 2008

FIGURE 13-1   Books for Story Reenactments.

What if more than one child wants the part of a character? Simply reenact the story again with a different set of characters. The more you do it, the better. Ishee and Goldhaber (1990) tell how their children performed **The Three Bears** 27 times in four days! Remember that repetition (mastery) is one of the 3-Ms of Self-Discovery (manipulation, mastery, and meaning) that most children use to make new experiences part of their repertoire. (See Strategy 19, "Alphabet.") Repeating the drama also helps shy children develop the courage to participate.

What about scenery? Story reenactments are not staged plays, and thus scenery or props are not necessary. However, it makes sense to use labeled chairs or tables to represent objects in the story when appropriate. These little dramas need to be as simple as possible so that children can perform them in an impromptu manner without a fuss. What if children forget their lines or their actions? Of course they will at first, because they perform without practicing. It is the *process* of making a story come alive that is most important, not the *product* of a finished play. Eventually, after you have read the story many times, certain children may have memorized the words and can even replace you as the "reader." Important benefits are gained by children from story reenactments when they learn:

- That words, not pictures, tell the story
- That words have different meanings
- A better "sense of story"
- That stories can come alive through acting
- That reading can be extended to other areas of the classroom
- That they will want you to reread the book
- That they can create their own stories
- That reading can be fun

Activities

*1. Read and reenact **My Name Is Not Isabella*** (Fosberry, J., 2010, Naperville, IL: Sourcebooks). Read this story several times if children are interested. The girls should be if you talk about it afterwards. This story can be reenacted by one girl who puts on a different hat as you read her accomplishments. Or different girls can take each of the different parts while another girl plays the mother character. Have hats and props ready before you start the drama. When her mother calls Isabella by each name, the girl responds, "My name is not . . ." Then she tells who she is and what she does—Sally Ride (astronaut), Annie Oakley (sharpshooter), Rosa Parks (civil rights activist), Marie Curie (scientist, inventor), and Elizabeth Blackwell (first woman doctor).

*2. Read and reenact **Giraffes Can't Dance*** (Andreae, G., 2001, New York: Orchard Books). All the children in your group or class can play the many jungle animal roles in this rhyming story after they become familiar with it. Gerald Giraffe was good at standing still and munching leaves off trees, but when he tried to run around, his knees buckled. He knew he would be unable to dance at the annual Jungle Dance. The warthogs were waltzing, the rhinos rock 'n' rolled, the lions tangoed, the chimps did the cha-cha, and the baboons reeled off a Scottish reel. But when Gerald tried to take a turn, they laughed him off the jungle floor. Back among the trees, a cricket told him he needed to find his own music: the swaying grass, the magic moon. Soon Gerald found his body shuffling, swaying, and dancing. The other animals said it was a miracle. Gerald said, "We all can dance when we find music that we love."

Have the children choose what animal they want to be and let them each make their moves to the snappy background music or jungle drums you play as you read the story. When Gerald finally takes the floor, have the others sit in a circle around him as he dances.

Your characters may want to make headbands with animal ears to wear for the reenactment. Another time have a small group reenact the story with only six children taking animal parts by dancing with large animal hand puppets. Lakeshore Learning Materials can supply large plush Big Mouth Jungle Puppets (Monkey, Rhino, Giraffe, Panda, Alligator, and Tiger) very reasonably, or children can make their own from paper bags or socks. You can adapt the story to the animals you have.

Another time, have the characters choose different types of music to dance to just as Gerald did. Try out several musical tapes or rhythms on xylophones or drums. Can the children make their own music with rhythm instruments?

SUGGESTED READINGS

Beaty, J. J., & Pratt, L. (2011). *Early literacy in preschool and kindergarten: A multicultural perspective.* 3rd ed. Boston: Pearson.

Ishee, N., & Goldhaber, J. (1990). Story re-enactment: Let the play begin! *Young Children, 45*(3), 70–75.

Meier, D. R. (Ed.). (2009). *Here's the story: Using narrative to promote young children's language and literacy learning.* New York: Teachers College Press.

Wannerman, T. (2010). Using story drama with young preschoolers. *Young Children, 65*(2), 20–28.

 Puppets

CONCEPT

Hand puppets in an early childhood classroom can be a most exciting prop for bringing children together with books. Your puppets can be the characters in the story who invite children to come and listen. If they are girl puppets, they can be Kristen who hurries to the zoo and rescues her baby brother from the gorilla, or Lola who will absolutely never eat a tomato. If they are boy puppets, they can be Lola's brother Charlie who tricks her into eating more than a tomato, or Filbert MacFee whose animal crackers turn the hospital into a zoo, or Tiny Tim who tries to eat his bathtub but it wouldn't go down his throat.

Bring in some animal puppets and your children can be the cow who types, the baby owl who wants his mother, or grumpy Gloria, the pudgy bulldog who feels left out when her little owner gets a new doll to play with. Excitement awaits anyone adventurous enough to put on a hand puppet!

Puppets Are Different for Young Children

Preschool children perceive puppets quite differently than do teachers or older children. Three- and 4-year-olds find it hard to understand the concept of a hand puppet as a doll that can speak and act. In fact, they do not treat puppets as they do their other dolls. Instead, they tend to see puppets on their hands as extensions of themselves rather than as separate objects. When they put on a hand puppet with a movable mouth, they often use it playfully to "bite" another child rather than to speak.

Puppet shows are another area of confusion for 3- and 4-year-olds. If they are asked to sit down in front of a puppet theater to watch a show, they tend to pop up and try to get hold of the puppets as soon as they appear. They are more interested in sticking their heads through the stage opening or running around in back to see what is going on back there. If they are asked to put on a puppet show themselves, they often stick their puppets far out of the stage opening, trying to touch someone in the audience.

Children can talk to one another with puppets.

Because their concept of "audience" is also not well developed, most young children are more comfortable using their puppets in other ways. Even the theater itself has little meaning for them at first. Left on their own, they may use a puppet theater as a pretend store. What will they sell? One group sold the puppets! But 5- and 6-year-olds tend to see puppets as adults do.

Teachers who understand about preschool children's use of puppets put away the puppet theater and encourage children to use puppets to tell stories. This they can do. Currenton (2006) notes: "Another way to encourage storytelling is to ask children to create fictional stories with puppets or dolls. One study found that children are better at retelling stories when they use dolls or puppets than when they use pictures of scenes from the story. Dolls and puppets allow children to tap into their pretend play skills" (p. 85).

Activities

1. Use puppets as book characters. When considering the use of puppets as book characters, it is essential to first select the appropriate books and reread them to the children several times. Introduce the puppets to one or two children at a time. You will need to serve as a model puppet character yourself so the children will see how a puppet takes on a role.

When choosing books for puppet role playing, be sure that they have short, memorable texts with repetition or rhyming that can be remembered easily. Young children will be able to recall characters if there are only one or two and if the dialogue between them is interesting.

2. Obtain the puppets. It is not necessary to have a puppet that looks exactly like a specific human character, although animal puppets are best that resemble specific animals. Hand puppets can be purchased or constructed by the teacher or children. Most children's book and toy stores now have hand puppets available. A good affordable source for animal puppets is in kitchen stores or kitchen departments where animal hot pad gloves are available in a variety of species. Educational supply companies have a good selection of hand puppets, such as the following from Lakeshore:

> Community Helpers Puppet Set
>
> Big Mouth Animal Puppet Pals
>
> Let's Talk Kid Puppet Set (multiethnic)
>
> Let's Talk Multicultural Puppet Set (Japanese, Mexican, Nigerian, Navajo, Ghanaian, Chinese)

Some of their puppets also go with specific books:

> **Goldilocks and the Three Bears**
>
> **The Three Little Pigs**
>
> **The Three Billy Goats Gruff**

3. Make your own puppets. To make your own hand puppets with the children, obtain small brown paper bags and show children how to put a face on the outside bottom end of the bag either with markers or eye stickers. Even simpler hand puppets can be made out of a sock worn over one hand with stickers for eyes.

*4. Read a simple book such as **I Love Bugs*** (Dodd, E., 2010, New York: Holiday House). Read the book several times with its wonderfully descriptive words: *slimy, creepy, spiky, fuzzy, stripy, swipey sting* bugs; *flouncy, frilly, flutter* bugs; *silly clitter-clutter* bugs. Have the children choose their favorite bug from the book and make a paper bag puppet of it. As you reread the book, have the children fly, stalk, creep, or walk their puppets around the room when they see their pictures as you turn the pages.

*5. Read a more complex book, **I Will Never Not Ever Eat a Tomato*** (Child, L., 2000, Cambridge, MA: Candlewick Press). Obtain or make puppets of Lola and her brother Charlie. Both of them have dialogue that you can read as children make motions with their puppets. Put out all of your plastic vegetables, fruit, and food items on the dramatic play table so that the Lola puppet can go around shaking her head at each one at first, and finally picking up each one and eating it when Charlie says things like: "These are not carrots. They are orange twiglets from Jupiter."

FIGURE 14–1 Charlie gets
Lola to eat a tomato.

After they have reenacted this story several times, some of your children may be able to repeat some of the puppets' lines. Also suggest that everyone draw pictures of the story (see Figure 14–1) and you will help make a book of them.

6. *Read the simple rhyming book **The Lady with the Alligator Purse*** (Westcott, N. B., 1988, Boston: Little, Brown). Children love this traditional call-for-the-doctor rhyme and soon will be shouting out in unison the words of the three puppet characters every time you pause after "the doctor said," "the nurse said," or "the lady said,"

> Doctor: "mumps," "penicillin"
>
> Nurse: "measles," "castor oil"
>
> Lady: "nonsense," "pizza"

Afterwards, choose three puppet characters and let them act as you read. Better have pizza ready for snack that day! Other fine books that can be used for puppet reenactments include:

> *Clarabella's Teeth* (Vrombaut, A., 2003, New York: Clarion Books)
>
> *Froggy Goes to the Doctor* (London, J., 2002, New York: Viking)
>
> *Grumpy Gloria* (Dewdney, A., 2006, New York: Viking)
>
> *I Am Not Sleepy and I Will Not Go to Bed* (Child, L., 2001, Cambridge, MA: Candlewick Press)
>
> *Llama Llama Home with Mama* (Dewdney, A., 2011, New York: Viking)
>
> *My Crayons Talk* (Hubbard, P., 1996, New York: Henry Holt)

SUGGESTED READINGS

Crepeau, I. M., & Richards, M. A. (2003). *A show of hands: Using puppets with children.* St. Paul, MN: Redleaf Press.

Currenton, S. M. (2006). Oral storytelling: A cultural art that promotes school readiness. *Young Children, 61*(5), 79–95.

Esch, G., & Long, E. (2002). The fabulous fun finger puppet workshop. *Young Children, 57*(1), 90–91.

15 Assessing Speaking Progress

CONCEPT

As mentioned previously, literacy for young children begins with speaking and listening to words. Brain research has shown that a baby's early nonverbal communication efforts help to wire her brain for the spoken and written language. By 6 months of age, the infant has become a language specialist, focused on the sounds she hears most frequently. By 20 months of age, children may have a sizable vocabulary—that is, if the adults around her have talked to one another and to her, as well as showing affection and interacting playfully. Children who have experienced little adult interaction or verbal communication are decidedly less verbal themselves. Thus the youngsters who come into your classroom may display a wide range of abilities in their knowledge and use of words. It is your goal to help all children at every level expand their vocabularies and develop confidence in their speaking abilities. Understanding and using words are, of course, the basis for young children's emergence into reading and writing.

What have you accomplished with individual children? It is important that you make an assessment of children's speaking progress. Although all the aspects of literacy—speaking, listening, reading, and writing—develop simultaneously, it is more expedient to assess them separately. Observing and recording individual children's speaking produces the best evidence of their growth and development.

Use a checklist to make an informal assessment of a child's listening and speaking.

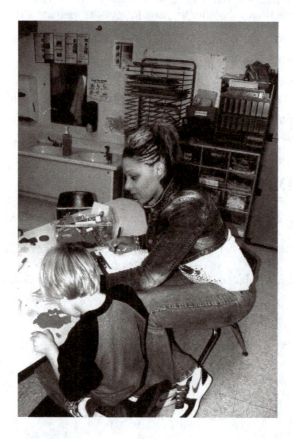

Activities

1. Start with a speaking behaviors checklist. It is important to observe and record a child's speaking behaviors using a checklist like the one shown in Figure 15–1 to learn the behaviors yourself. Not only will you know what to look for in individual children, but you will be able to make plans for activities to help all children. As you observe each child using a checklist, be sure to reproduce several copies of the checklist to be taped to cards that you give to staff members to help complete the observations.

2. Read books that feature children's self-concept for children who seldom speak. See Figure 15–2 for an excellent list of self-concept books. Some children may speak fluently at home, but are too shy to say much in the classroom. In that case, you will know that the most important activities you can arrange for them will be confidence builders: reading books that feature children's self-concept and planning activities in which they can succeed and be acknowledged for their success. Using pressure to get them to speak will produce the opposite results. Talk with their parents about how much they are speaking at home and how you are encouraging them to participate in classroom projects. Be sure to mention the positive things their children are accomplishing. If some children seem overwhelmed by the size of the class, pair them with an appropriate book buddy to help them become involved in fun activities two can enjoy.

Name_____ Age_____
Observer_____ Dates_____
_____Listens but seldom speaks
_____Speaks with single-words answers
_____Speaks in short phrases
_____Speaks in expanded sentences
_____Takes part in conversations
_____Asks questions
_____Does chanting, singing, finger plays
_____Speaks in dramatic play role
_____Speaks for a doll, puppet
_____Says rhyming words
_____Tells picture caption to teacher
_____Tells story from a book

FIGURE 15–1   Speaking Behaviors Checklist.

Incredible Me! (Appelt, K., 2003)
You Can Do It! (Dungy, T., 2008)*
I Can Do It Too! (Baicker, K., 2003)*
I Like Myself! (Beaumont, K., 2004)*
I Can Do Anything That's Everything All On My Own (Child, L., 2008)
I'm Gonna Like Me (Curtis, J. L., 2002)
Wow! It Sure Is Good to Be You! (Jabar, C., 2006)*
I Can Be Anything! (Spinelli, J., 2010)

_____
* multicultural

FIGURE 15–2   Self-Concept Books.

Sometimes children who seldom speak have a hearing impairment. If you surmise that this is the case, talk with the parents about having their child tested.

3. Make an audio tape of the child speaking to a staff member and to another child, or record the child's storytelling. It is important to obtain baseline data, such as an audio recording tape of the child's talking, when she first enters the program and later when she has participated in a variety of speaking activities. This will help you to decide which activities are most effective in promoting her growth in this area.

4. Tape record an informal interview you conduct with the child on a pretend phone call. Analyze the recording you make to see how the child is progressing in her speaking. Does she answer your questions with only one word or with expanded sentences? Can she keep up her end of a conversation with you? Be sure the interview is informal and fun.

From these assessment activities you should be able to interpret what each child's speaking strengths and needs are. Then you will be able to plan activities to support the child's speaking progress. Start from her strengths. If she likes playing with puppets, bring in more puppets and choose one or two other children to play puppets with her. You can tape record their "puppet talk" and play it back for them. Can they make up a story for their puppets? One thing leads to another in early childhood classrooms if teachers keep their eyes and ears open for what is going on with the children. Even shy children eventually respond to activities that involve their special interests.

SUGGESTED READINGS

Beaty, J. J. (2010). *Observing development of the young child.* 7th ed. Upper Saddle River, NJ: Merrill/ Prentice Hall.

Enz, B. J., & Morrow, L. M. (2009). *Assessing preschool literacy development.* Newark, DE: International Reading Association.

Jalongo, M. R. (2007). *Learning to listen, listening to learn.* Washington, DC: National Association for the Education of Young Children (NAEYC).

Part 2

Children's Writing

16 Emergent Writing

CONCEPT

Young children's first writing is scribbling. They scribble up and down and around with pencils, markers, chalk, paintbrushes, and even their fingers. Most adults tend to disregard this early stage of writing, saying, "Oh, it's only scribbling." But scribbling is to writing what babbling is to speaking, an early stage of children's development that should be encouraged. As they continue to scribble, children begin to notice what they are doing. As their hands and fingers become stronger and they are better able to control their scribbling implement, their scribbles begin to evolve into shapes: circles, ovals, squares, and crosses, among others, one on top of the other.

Soon they are making scribbles that cover the middle of their paper, adding another line of scribbles underneath. This is the beginning of their differentiation between picture scribbles and writing scribbles. Sometimes they will pretend to read this pretend writing. Other times they may bring their "picture" over to you and ask you to read what it is about. Because you know how to read and they

As young children's hands and fingers grow stronger they are better able to control the scribbles they make.

don't, they assume you will be able to translate their linear writing scribbles. Simply tell them you used to be able to read scribble writing, but now you have forgotten how. Maybe they can tell you what it says.

If we want young children to take their early writing efforts seriously, we need to treat them seriously as well. It is better not to tell them these early efforts are "scribbles," which sounds too babyish. Kissel (2009) talks about the preschool writers in a class he visited: "The children in Ronda's class used the term 'writing' to describe what they did on the page. They used symbols, lines, shapes, letter-like figures, letters, spoken words, movements, and drawings to convey intentional messages. As their awareness of letters and print grew, additional letters crept into their writing. By the end of the year, children labeled drawings with letters" (p. 161).

Their early lines of writing, however, looked nothing like letters or words at first. Learning to write is not only a lengthy and complex process, but it is much different from what logic tells us it ought to be. It would seem that learning to write is simply learning to make letters and combine them into words. Research has proven otherwise. Rather than mastering the parts (letters) first, children do just the opposite. They attend to the whole (written lines) first, and much later to the parts (letters) (Temple, Nathan, & Burris, 1993, p. 19).

Child development of all kinds proceeds from the general to the specific like this. In motor development, the large muscles of children's arms and legs develop before the small muscles of their fingers and hands and their toes and feet. In drawing, most children make generic humans who all look alike before they begin to draw specific people with identifying characteristics.

In writing, children first see the whole pattern (lines across a page), and only later can they identify separate words and finally letters. They are at the "emergent stage" in learning to write. From their own observations, and not from being taught, they seem to extract the broad general features of the writing system: that it is arranged in rows across a page; that it consists of loops, sticks, and connected lines, repeated over and over. Some children fill pages of scribbled lines over and over from top to bottom in a sort of self-imposed practice level. Kissel (2009) concluded: "When pre-kindergarten children write, the message they commit to the page exists at intersections where talk, movement, and image converge" (p. 161).

Eventually you will note that alphabet-like cursive letters ("mock letters") begin to appear in their lines of scribbles. When children begin to write mostly lines of letters ("letter strings"), they may again ask you to read them, as previously noted. If given enough time and support, children will create their own knowledge about writing by extracting the information from the writing they see around them. It is not up to you to teach formal writing to preschool children. Instead, you should observe the kinds of scribble writing and mock writing they are doing and encourage them to continue by providing outlets for their writing: sign-up sheets, journals, messages, signs, lists, and stories.

Printing is somewhat different from the cursive writing described above. Children also go through several emergent stages in teaching themselves to print letters and words with the letters in order. Even the letters of their names are sometimes mixed up, written backwards, upside down, or scattered around a page. (See Figure 16–1.) The concept of a "word" is still somewhat fuzzy for them, and they often substitute the picture of an object for the word. It is not for you to correct them but to encourage them by involving them in all kinds of writing. What they need is the freedom and time to experiment on their own. They will eventually get it right. As Temple et al. tell us, "It appears that we learn to write at least as much by discovering as by being taught. Learning to write is largely an act of discovery" (p. 2).

Some child development specialists are worried that teachers who are unfamiliar with the concept of emergent writing may not know how to help these children. As Schrader and Hoffman (1987) note: "When teachers are unfamiliar with current knowledge about the natural development of literacy in young children, they impose skill-oriented expectations and tasks on these youngsters—copying and tracing standard adult print, for example. Such activities not only are stressful for 3-, 4-, and 5-year-old children, but they do not afford children the opportunity to use their self-constructed knowledge in meaningful ways" (p. 13).

FIGURE 16–1 This child drew and wrote about her favorite foods with the only letters she knew written backwards.

Activities

1. Observe samples of children's writing on a daily basis using a checklist. You will want to know how far along each of the children have progressed in their emergence into writing. Observe samples of their writing on a daily basis and use the checklist in Figure 16–2 to help you determine where they stand. You may find that some children skip some of the items listed while others seem to be stuck doing the same type of writing over and over. Don't forget that repetition like this is part of the natural progression and should be expected. Others may progress in an entirely different manner. Accept whatever they do and encourage them to continue in the many exciting writing activities you provide.

EARLY CHILDHOOD WRITING BEHAVIORS

Child's Name_____ Age____ Date_____
_____Scribbles in a line across a page
_____Scribbles in a line under drawing scribbles
_____Fills pages with lines of writing-like scribbles
_____Makes a few mock letters in lines of scribbles
_____Makes more mock letters and fewer scribble marks
_____Makes printed letters here and there, some reversed
_____Prints letters of first name but not in order, some reversed
_____Prints first name, letters in order
_____Prints other words along with pictures

FIGURE 16–2 Checklist for Early Writing Behaviors.

```
┌─────────────────────────────────────────────────────────────┐
│   Get-well cards              Signs for block buildings       │
│   Messages                    Journals                        │
│   Lists of ingredients        Permission slips                │
│   Lists of pets               Thank-you notes                 │
│   Sign-up sheets              Stories                         │
│   Birthday cards              Story (picture) captions         │
│   Mother's and Father's Day cards                             │
└─────────────────────────────────────────────────────────────┘
```

FIGURE 16–3   Authentic Writing Activities.

2. Involve children in writing activities that are purposeful but fun. Writing should be fun for these children and not a chore. But there should be a purpose behind it, as well. Some of the authentic writing activities the children can be involved in (even if they only scribble) are shown in Figure 16–3.

3. Read books in which characters are involved in writing. Read books to small groups or individuals in which the characters are involved in writing, and invite your children to reenact the stories, including the writing parts. The following books are important ones to obtain (either directly from the publishers or from a library) because they are simple, fast-moving, and funny enough for preschool youngsters to want to hear them again and again. Then they can choose the animal and human roles with glee for story reenactments as you read the words. But be sure to let Ruby, Max, and the duck print or scribble their own notes as best they can.

*4. Read **Bunny Cakes** (Wells, R., 1997, New York: Dial Books).* Little bunny Max decides to make his grandma an earthworm birthday cake. But his older sister Ruby informs him they are going to make an angel surprise cake with raspberry-fluff icing. Max tries to help but only creates a mess and is sent to the store several times with a list of ingredients to replace. Ruby carefully prints EGGS in black crayon the first time, but Max adds his own ingredients ("Red-Hot Marshmallow Squirters") as a huge red crayon scribble. The grocer gives Max eggs. When he has to return for milk, Max tries writing about the squirters in red and green, but still the grocer can't read the scribbles. In the end, Max draws a picture of two Red-Hot Marshmallow Squirters and the grocer finally understands.

*5. Read **Giggle, Giggle, Quack** (Cronin, D., 2002, New York: Simon & Schuster).* Here is another hilarious Farmer Brown story. This time the farmer goes on vacation, leaving his brother Bob in charge of the animals with the warning to follow his written instructions, but to keep an eye on the duck: he's trouble. Duck finds a pencil and begins writing his own instructions for Bob about getting pizza for the hens, washing the pigs with bubble bath, and getting a video movie, "The Sound of Moosic," for the cows. When Farmer Brown calls home and hears the giggles, moos, oinks, and a quack as hen picks up the phone, he knows what has happened. Duck writes his last note: "It's for you, Bob!"

SUGGESTED READINGS

Hughes, E., & Wineman, K. (2009). Learning language: Listening and writing with diverse young children. *Dimensions of Early Childhood, 37*(2), 3–8.

Kissel, B. T. (2009). Beyond the page: Peers influence pre-kindergarten writing through image, movement, and talk. *Childhood Education, 85*(3), 160–166.

Schrader, C. T., & Hoffman, S. (1987). Encouraging children's early writing efforts. *Day Care and Early Education, 15*(2), 9–13.

Shagoury, R. (2009). Language to language: Nurturing writing development in multilingual classrooms. *Young Children, 64*(2), 52–57.

Temple, C. A., Nathan, R. G., & Burris, N. A. (1993). *The beginnings of writing.* Boston: Allyn & Bacon.

Writing Center

CONCEPT

One of the important literacy-focused areas of every early childhood classroom should be the writing center. Such a center can take a number of sizes and configurations. Some writing centers have a scaled-down business desk and chairs as well as nearby shelves full of writing materials. Others may look like a full-fledged office with a computer, typewriter, phone, filing cabinet, tables for writing, and a bulletin board. Some may take the form of a post office with letter boxes, mail slots, and tables for writing and stamping envelopes. One class made theirs into a newspaper office with desks for the reporters, a typewriter, computer, and stacks of newspapers and magazines.

Vukelich and Christie (2009) tell how some teachers put the writing center in a section of the book (library) center. In it they put a table, chairs, writing tools, and small blank books to encourage children to write books or in journals. No matter what it looks like, the presence of a writing center says something significant to the children: writing is important in this classroom.

Be sure you fill your writing center with many kinds of writing materials that you change from time to time. Variety is as important to young children as it is to adults. Figure 17–1 shows a number of writing tools and materials.

Activities

1. Involve children in using the typewriter. Filling your writing center with supplies is the same as stocking your art center with painting supplies. Make sure the materials are authentic and not children's toy implements. Youngsters want to use real equipment and be engaged in authentic activities. An adult typewriter, for instance, is always preferred to a child's toy typewriter. Old, standard manual typewriters are often available from used office equipment dealers or parents. Although children often play around with a typewriter at first, eventually they learn by trial and error to press the keys without jamming them. Letters on the keys become meaningful when they learn to press them one at a time to type their names.

This boy learns to press one typewriter key at a time in the writing center.

Pencils	Pens and Markers	Rubber Stamps	Paper
Regulation size	Rolling writers	Alphabet letters	Typing paper
Primary size	Felt-tip markers	Animal stamps	Notebooks
Colored	Various colors	Address stamps	Stationery
Automatic	Chalk, chalkboard	Peel-offs	Colored paper
Miscellaneous			
Pencil sharpener	Paper clips	Glue, paste	Stencils
Stapler, staples	Hole puncher	Cellophane tape	Stamps

FIGURE 17–1   Writing Tools and Materials.

What else can they type? Simple messages are the easiest, although some experienced "typists" will want to write simple stories. Be sure you read to them the comical book **Click, Clack, Moo: Cows That Type** (Cronin, D., 2000, New York: Simon & Schuster), about the cows that find an old typewriter in the barn and type Farmer Brown a message about being cold and wanting electric blankets. Can your typists type a message (invented spelling is fine) about what they want to do next?

2. *Start a sign-making shop.* Children who enjoy writing can make signs to be used around the classroom. The block building center, for instance, often needs signs that say Stop, One-Way, Zoo, Please Don't Touch, or Save This Building. Other areas also need label signs saying Dramatic Play, Music, Art, Manipulatives, Water Table, Science, or Waste Paper Here. The book center may need sign-out cards for the books or literacy bags children will be taking home, as well as sign-up clipboards for the computer or tape player.

3. *Put together writing bags full of supplies for home.* Your writing center can contain plastic bags and cases or backpacks of writing supplies you have assembled for overnight lending. Children can borrow these cases to be used at home and returned the next day just as they do with duplicate paperback picture books that you circulate to the homes. Many parents may not be aware of their children's desire and need to communicate in writing at this early age. Send home some of their classroom writing as well, and ask the parents to share some of the writing their children do at home. Remember, this should be a pleasurable activity, not a chore or homework.

4. *Create a post office.* Make your writing center into a post office with a painted shoe box or cereal box for each child's letters. Have them make their own. Have canceled stamps, rubber stampers and ink pads, and a counter for children to use with their letters. Read the classic Keats book **A Letter to Amy** (1968, New York: Puffin) about Peter, who writes a letter inviting Amy to his birthday party and takes it outside to mail it, but it blows away in the rain.

SUGGESTED READINGS

Beaty, J. J., & Pratt, L. (2011). *Early literacy in preschool and kindergarten: A multicultural perspective.* 3rd ed. Boston: Pearson.

Brown, K. M. (2010). Young authors: Writing workshop in kindergarten. *Young Children, 65*(1), 24.

Schickedanz, J. A., & Casbergue, R. M. (2009). *Writing in preschool: Learning to orchestrate meaning and marks.* Newark, DE: International Reading Association.

Vukelich, C., & Christie, J. (2009). *Building a foundation for preschool literacy: Effective instruction for children's reading and writing development.* Newark, DE: International Reading Association.

18 Environmental Print

CONCEPT

Environmental print includes the signs, slogans, logos, and printed words located in the children's environment. It consists of billboards, traffic signs, fast-food restaurant signs, labels on cereal boxes and food containers in supermarkets, signs on buses, slogans on T-shirts and even children's pajamas, and the many signs and labels on the items and walls of their classroom. Reading specialists have discovered that children learn to "read" this familiar printed matter seen around them on a daily basis long before they recognize the words in a book. They are, of course, memorizing these words from hearing what others call them and from seeing them over and over. For many children they are an important doorway into emergent reading and writing.

Despite the commercial aspects of some of it, outside environmental print can contribute to young children's emergent reading and writing ability in the classroom. There seems to be more such environmental print outside many classrooms than inside. Xu and Rutledge (2003) point out that young children may not read the letters of the logos at first, but rely on contextual clues to help them understand the names: "For example, McDonald's familiar arch shape and golden color—and possibly its big M—create a meaningful context for children to recognize the McDonald's logo as signifying a favorite place to eat" (p. 44). Using the lists in Figure 18–1, think of ways you can bring some of this print into the daily activities of the various classroom learning centers. Be sure to point to classroom signs and have children guess what they say.

Environmental print in this classroom is on the walls. Here are a calendar and the names of days of the week in Spanish.

Dramatic Play Center	**Block Center**	**Science Center**	**Music Center**
Chair, table, oven labels	Unit blocks	Aquarium	Tape recorder
Empty cereal boxes	Trucks	Terrarium	Tapes
Milk cartons	People	Pet cage	Headsets
Food wrappers	Dinosaurs	Ant farm	Rhythm
Bread wrappers	Traffic signs	Collections	Instruments
Hamburger wrappers	Store signs		

FIGURE 18–1   Some Classroom Environmental Print.

Activities

1. Place environmental print in the dramatic play center. Send home a note to parents asking them to look around their kitchen for words their children know, like "milk" on a milk carton, the name of a cereal they eat, or a bread wrapper. Ask them to bring these empty items to school. Collect print items yourself from your own kitchen, a fast-food restaurant, as well as old magazines, toy catalogs, or a phone book. Set up a restaurant, a food store, or a kitchen in the dramatic play center, using the print items you have collected. Wrap unit blocks with food wrappers you have collected (e.g., hamburger wrappers or breakfast bar wrappers). As children play in the pretend restaurant, store, or kitchen, have them try to recognize the words of the logos. Have children try making their own signs using the ones they have as models.

2. Place environmental print in the block center. Take the children on a field trip outside the building and down the street. Make it a "treasure hunt" for signs. Carry a camera and take photos of the signs they see: stop signs, street names, store names, bumper stickers, gas station, direction signs (One Way), warning signs (No Trespassing), license plates, and parking signs. Enlarge the photos, cut out the signs, and mount them on cardboard for play in the block center. Or copy them on block center signs that children can use in their play. Use duplicate signs for matching games.

3. Take children on a field trip to a zoo or aquarium. Look for and copy down signs throughout the buildings and grounds, naming the animals you are looking at. Afterwards, make similar signs for the block center and encourage the children to build a zoo or aquarium for their plastic land or aquatic animals. Read books about the zoos or aquariums. If the books contain signs naming the animals, see if the children can name the signs. If the books show no signs, see if your listeners can identify the sign they made for each zoo or aquarium animal when you come to the page describing the animal.

*4. Read **Carlo Likes Reading** (Spanyol, J., 2001, Cambridge, MA: Candlewick).* All the items in Carlo's bedroom are labeled with tags, as are all the items in his kitchen (which is set for breakfast), all the items in his bathroom, all the items in his living room, all the items in his playroom, all the items in his garage, all the items outside in his yard (including ants and stones), all the items on the street outside a bakery shop, all the items in the park, and all the items in a vegetable market. Obviously, your children should not be expected to name all or even many of these items. Instead, take one room at a time and see if individuals can guess the name on the label by recognizing the item. Next time you look at the story with the same children, choose a different room in the book and have them guess the names.

5. Place environmental naming signs throughout the classroom. Now it is time to begin labeling objects in your classroom. Be sure they are at the children's eye level. Have file cards cut to size, markers, and tape ready for use. Ask the first small group which five objects in the classroom should be labeled. Make labels in a second language if you serve Dual Language Learners. Have children help make labels and stick them to the objects. Have the next groups each choose five objects they want to have labeled. The next time you read **Carlo Likes Reading**, ask the listeners to find objects in Carlo's pages with the same labels as those in the classroom. It is too confusing to put as many labels on things as in the book. It is more important for you and the children to get involved with doing the labeling and having them guess what the labels say. Otherwise they may pay no attention to the labels.

6. *Match labels and objects.* Some of the children may be able to match label cards from a duplicate set you have made with objects in the classroom. Put out a few label cards on a table and see if the children can match any of them to the labels around the room. Make it fun.

SUGGESTED READINGS

Davidson, J. I. (1996). *Emergent literacy and dramatic play in early education.* Clifton Falls, New York: Delmar.

Strickland, D. S., & Schickedanz, J. A. (2009). *Learning about print in preschool: Working with letters, words, and beginning links with phonemic awareness.* 2nd ed. Newark, DE: International Reading Association.

West, L. S., & Egley, E. H. (1998). Children get more than a hamburger: Using labels and logos to enhance literacy. *Dimensions of Early Childhood, 26*(3–4), 43–46.

Xu, S. H., & Rutledge, A. L. (2003). Kindergartners learn through environmental print. *Young Children, 58*(2), 45–49.

Alphabet

CONCEPT

Research suggests that a child's knowledge of the alphabet is one of the best predictors of her success in early reading. As Strickland and Schickedanz (2009) tell us, "Letter name, or alphabet knowledge, is an excellent predictor of success in early reading" (p. 4). Does this mean you should teach preschool children the alphabet before they enter kindergarten so they will have a head start on learning to read and write? Not at all. Young children learn letters, numbers, and concepts of all kinds on their own by playing around with them and using them in all sorts of ways—not by being formally taught. As Strickland and Schickedanz (2009) conclude, "Simply training children to memorize letters without providing learning in a larger literacy context has proven unsuccessful as a predictor of beginning reading success" (p. 4).

Teaching preschool children to memorize all the letters is not developmentally appropriate. After all, it is not the entire alphabet itself that children need to learn at this age, but *letters from the alphabet that they find useful*. As Neuman, Copple, and Bredekamp (2000) point out, "Long before they go to school, young children can learn to spot letters important to them, such as the 'S' in Sesame Street or the 'Z' of zoo" (p. 65). Often the first letter of their name is the letter they recognize first. This learning is known as the *alphabetic principle*.

Self-Discovery Play

Because young children learn through play, it is useful for the teacher to recognize the levels of "self-discovery play" all children everywhere seem to progress through on their own. We call these levels "the 3-Ms of Self-Discovery": manipulation, mastery, and meaning. When children encounter a new object, say a toy telescope, they first of all *manipulate* it. They open it and close it, look through it backwards, roll it across the table, or even bang it on a pan as a drumstick.

These girls accidentally found a "W"—or is it an "M"?

Letter blocks to transport in toy trucks
Magnetic letters to line up on a metal cabinet door
Beanbag letters to toss at a target
Sponge letters for dipping in paint and stamping
Lacing bead letters to string on a necklace
Pretzels to break off pieces to make letters

FIGURE 19–1   Letters to Play With.

When they finally discover how the telescope really works and what it can be used for, they pull it open, look at something through it, and close it. Then they repeat this action over and over. This is the *mastery* level, a sort of self-imposed practice. Finally, many but not all youngsters progress to the *meaning* level, where they make the object meaningful to them. Perhaps they go outside and look through it at a bird in a tree, or incorporate it into a dramatic play episode as a captain of a ship looking for land.

Can children play with alphabet letters like this? They can if you provide them with three-dimensional letters and give them an opportunity to experiment on their own. They may or may not use them as suggested. They may *manipulate* them by standing them on end or piling them up. They may exhibit *mastery* by lining up the same letters over and over. They may display *meaning* by lining up the letters of their name.

Keep your eyes open for their own games and ideas. But don't forget to comment on what you see the children doing with the letters. "Oh, Randy, what a great tower you built out of all the 'A' blocks!" Or "Jessica, do you know what you're feeding your baby dolls? Beanbag letter sandwiches! I see a 'P' and an 'O' and a 'T.'" Or "Jake, you have stamped a 'J' on your napkin. Do you know that's the first letter of your name, J-A-K-E?"

It is up to the teacher of young children to supply the classroom with a variety of three-dimensional alphabet letters that they can play with. Remember, preschool children have not yet learned to identify many of the 26 letters by name. Activities like those shown in Figure 19–1 should help them proceed through the self-discovery play levels and identify more letters. Once they know a few letters they are delighted to find them in new places. The two girls in the photo playing with building logs accidentally moved them so they formed a "W," which the first girl noted. But the second girl insisted it was an "M" for her name, Marcella. As their teacher, what would you have said?

Alphabet Books

Strickland and Schickedanz (2009) tell us that "regular exposure to alphabet books during read-aloud time is essential to supporting children's learning of letter names" (p. 73). Such books for children of preschool age (3 to 5 years old) are much more abstract than the three-dimensional letters they are playing with. This means that after reading the books, you should do something playful with the three-dimensional letters and ideas presented by the books. The books should be bright, lively, and tell a fast-paced story if you want children to look at them. They should contain the criteria noted in Figure 19–2. Letters should stand out and be clearly related to objects that the children are familiar with.

These books present preschool children with an entirely new concept: that a letter of the alphabet represents an object. It is a concept not easily understood by young children at first, yet they do seem to memorize the fact that "A" stands for "Apple" because you say so. They may wonder, "Why should it?" since "A" does not look or sound anything like Apple. Remember, most preschool children are concerned with the *sounds of the names* of letters (ay), not the sound the letter makes. That will come later when they begin to recognize words.

FIGURE 19–2   Choosing Alphabet Books for Preschool Children.

- One large letter to a page
- Colorful objects that children recognize
- A fast-paced story or theme that rhymes
- A lead-in to hands-on activities

If you have one or two alphabet books in your classroom, you should read them to only a few children at a time. Then they can sit close enough to see the pictures and begin to catch on that letters represent objects or actions on the page. Later they can look at the books on their own. Use each book (not worksheets) as a lead-in to three-dimensional, hands-on activities based on it.

Activities

1. Read **Alphabet Under Construction** (Fleming, D., 2003, New York: Holt). Mouse works his way through each huge letter on a page, airbrushing, buttoning, and carving every one. Have your listeners sit close so they can get ideas for decorating their own letters. Put out a set of white cutout letters and a basket of collage materials (buttons, sequins, tiny shells, macaroni shapes, feathers), along with colored markers and glue sticks, and have each child choose and decorate his or her own letter.

2. Read **L M N O Peas** (Baker, K., 2010, New York: Beach Lane Books). Children love to sing the alphabet song. Does this teach them the letters? Not really. Listen closely and you will hear them sing the line "L, M, N, O, P" as one word, not separate letters.

Baker has written an alphabet book based on this phrase. His "alphabet peas" are tiny people who work and play in giant ABCs. For example, the A's are acrobats, artists, and astronauts. The last page asks the reader, "Who are you?" Ask the children who they would like to be. Then go back through the book and help them find their letter. This is not as simple as it seems for children. Someone may want to be a doctor, for instance, but have no idea what letter doctor begins with.

3. Read **B Is for Bulldozer: A Construction ABC** (Sobel, J., 2003, San Diego: Harcourt). Read this book before or after a field trip to a construction or a road repair site. A rhyming sentence on each page shows pieces of construction equipment with their first letter in color: **C**rane, **D**ump truck, **F**orklift. Afterwards, take the book and a sheet of peel-off letters to the block building center to see if children can find any of this equipment on the block accessory shelves. Let the finder stick on its peel-off letter.

4. Read **Chicka Chicka Boom Boom** (Martin, B., & Archambault, J., 1989, New York: Simon & Schuster). This classic story will always remain a favorite. The letters themselves talk in rhyme: "A told B, and B told C, I'll meet you at the top of the coconut tree." Then they wonder: "Chicka, chicka, boom, boom! Will there be enough room?" Children love to repeat the catchy verses and afterwards to play a game that you make up in which everyone falls down. Children can each carry a letter and march to a center spot in your room until it becomes so crowded that everyone falls down. Or you can make your own tree, wrap it in a brown towel, and march Velcro letters up to the top until it gets too full. Constructive Playthings offers a 20-inch freestanding cloth tree with letters, along with a CD containing songs, rhymes, and fun.

5. Read **N is for Navidad** (Elya, S. M., 2007, San Francisco, CA: Chronicle Books). Here is a Spanish alphabet celebrating the Christmas season with letters representing Spanish words, but with their rhyming story in English. A is for Angel, B is for Buenuelos (flat, fried pastries), C is for Campanas (bells), and so forth—all the way to Z for Zapatos (shoes set out the night before the Three Kings Day). Every colorful page shows an excited Hispanic family celebrating the 22 days of this holiday. Hispanic children in the class may want to tell how their families celebrate this holiday. Children from other cultures can learn what Hispanic children do.

SUGGESTED READINGS

Neuman, S. B., Copple, C., & Bredekamp, S. (2000). *Learning to read and write*. Washington, DC: National Association for the Education of Young Children.

Strickland, D. S., & Schickedanz, J. A. (2009). *Learning about print in preschool: Working with letters, words, and beginning links with phonemic awareness*. 2nd ed. Newark, DE: International Reading Association.

Wuori, D. (1999). Beyond the letter of the week: Authentic literacy comes to kindergarten. *Young Children, 54*(6), 24–25.

Names

CONCEPT

Children's names have long been an important part of early childhood learning and teaching. Not only do they identify the children for the teaching staff and their classmates, but they also identify the children for themselves. Children who enter the program at age 3 may still have a rather shaky image of who they are. Suddenly they hear their name called, not once but many times, by the teachers and their classmates. When they hear their name they respond to it. This is who they are: Allison, Jennifer, Kaitlyn, Megan, Melissa, Shandra, or Yolanda; Brandon, Dylan, Jesse, Keshawn, Kyle, Miguel, Travis, or Tyrone. People ask them what their names are and they tell them with confidence. Children also like to hear their names sung in greeting songs, good-bye songs, getting-ready songs, and pick-up songs to familiar tunes such as "Lazy Mary":

Keshawn Williams, will you pick up,

Will you pick up, will you pick up,

Keshawn Williams, will you pick up,

The blocks and trucks today.

Then they begin seeing their names written on name tags, placemats, circle time mats, cubbies, crayon boxes, artwork, toothbrushes, blankets, and computer printouts. Soon they recognize that those printed symbols are also who they are. Names seem to be their personal property. Those written names identify things that belong to them.

Using only uppercase letters is best at first. Children do seem to find it easier to write uppercase letters. However, the print they see in books contains both upper- and lowercase letters. Exposure to both kinds of print helps them become accustomed to both. Next the teachers want them to write their own names on artwork, writing paper, and sign-up sheets. Some children have already learned at home how to write their names. But many newcomers have not. If you have a mixed-age class, the 5-year-olds may have had more experience with writing names than the 3-year-olds. But now everyone is encouraged to print their names, at least the first letter.

Learning to Write Their Names

Teachers may help at first. In years past, teachers often printed out children's names in upper- and lowercase and had them trace them over and over with a marker or their finger. Today some teachers give each child a card with his name printed in large letters for him or her to copy onto another paper. At first children try to copy and later generate their names on their own. Some generate without copying. Some just scribble at first. But many children seem to trace spontaneously without being instructed, and then copy their names.

Children have heard their names pronounced aloud. Now they are learning that their names can be written down. They must be words—like the words on the labels for objects in the classroom. For many children their names are the first word they learn to recognize by sight. As Kirk and Clark (2005) note, "Almost every language skill necessary to learning to read can be introduced by using children's names" (p. 139).

FIGURE 20–1 Kayelynn prints letters of her first and last name at the top of her drawing.

FIGURE 20–2 Steps toward Children Writing Their First Names.

- Children recognize their spoken names.
- Children recognize their written names.
- Children experiment scribbling their names.
- Children trace, copy, or generate name letters.
- Children print their name in proper order.
- Children select their name card by first letter alone.
- Children learn names of letters in their names.
- Children use letters in their names to write other words.

Children learn to print the letters in their names even before they know the names of the letters. At first they may omit a letter or scatter the letters around on the paper, sometimes backwards or upside down as Kayelynn did in her Figure 20–1 drawing. Although it may take awhile, finally they get it right, usually in the steps shown in Figure 20–2. They then have a repertory of known letters, letters that can be used to write other words.

In the beginning, only the first letter of a child's name may be familiar. When teachers put out the name cards of everyone in the class and ask children to find theirs, Megan may pick up Melissa's card because she recognizes only the first letter. Remembering that young children start with the general and then learn the specific, you could have Megan compare her name card with Melissa's, having her note that Melissa's name starts with the same letter as hers but Melissa's name is longer. Children eventually memorize the names of the letters in their names and how to write them. Now they are ready to use these same letters for recognizing and writing other words.

Activities

1. Play games to help children recognize letters by their names. Have a variety of solid letter sets (such as wood, plastic, magnetic, and cardboard) that can be used in matching games and alphabet dominoes. Have each of the children become a letter they know and go around the room finding objects (labeled or not) that begin with their letter.

Play a follow-the-directions game in which you have children holding a letter card sit in chairs in a circle while you call out directions: "b's wiggle both your feet," or "h's shake hands with a's," or "j's jump up and down" or "c's clap your hands."

*2. Read **Eleanor, Ellatony, Ellencake, and Me*** (Rubin, C. M., 2003, Columbus, OH: McGraw-Hill Children's Publishing). In this humorous rhyming story Eleanor starts out with one name, but then each member of her family calls her something different: Elle, Nana's precious belle; Punch, Grandpa's playmate; Eleanora, Dad's movie star; Ellatony, Mom's little elbow macaroni. Finally she rebels and decides that she will be Ellie and nothing else, and so she is. Show the children how you can change Ellie's name with magnetic letters. Start with Eleanor and then go through the different changes in the story. Can your listeners tell which is which? Have one listener at a time try writing her own name in magnetic letters. Children are often sensitive about their names or nicknames, so tread carefully about changing theirs even in fun.

*3. Read **Harry and the Dinosaurs Go to School*** (Whybrow, I., 2006, New York: Random House). Harry takes his bucket of dinosaurs to school where he introduces them by their dinosaur names to a new boy, and they both make picture labels for their coat pegs. Your children can do the same. Will some be able to write their names on their labels?

Names in Diverse Languages

Some of the multiethnic children in your class may write their names in an alphabet different from English. You may want to read picture books showing these letters.

*4. Read **My Name Is Yoon*** (Recorvits, H., 2003, New York: Frances Foster Books). Yoon is a little Korean girl who has come to America with her family. When her father tells her she must learn to write her name YOON with English letters—lines, circles, each standing alone, she does not like it. The Korean character of her name looks happier. It means "shining warrior." In school when she has to sign her papers she tries out different names: CAT, BIRD, and even CUPCAKE. Her teacher accepts Yoon and every name she writes. Then one day she signs her paper YOON on every line. Her teacher gives her a big hug. But even in English Yoon still means shining warrior.

*5. Read **The Day of Ahmed's Secret*** (Heide, F. P., & Gilliland, J. H., 1990, New York: Lothrop, Lee, & Shepard Books). Ahmed, an Egyptian boy in the city of Cairo, works all day carrying heavy bottles of fuel on his donkey cart to his customers around the city. On the day of this story he also carries a secret that he tells no one until he arrives home at day's end. There he pulls out a piece of paper for his family to see. On it is his name written in Arabic. He has learned to write his name! Have your listeners look closely at the name and then at the city scenes to see if they can find other examples of signs in Arabic.

*6. Read **Mama Says: A Book of Love for Mothers and Sons*** (Walker, R. D., 2009, New York: The Blue Sky Press). This wonderful book shows a full-page illustration of each mother speaking to her son in twelve different languages opposite a short saying from each mama, translated into her alphabet. The languages are: Cherokee, Russian, Amharic (Ethiopia), Japanese, Hindi (India), Inuktitut (Alaskan Inuit), Hebrew, English, Korean, Arabic, Quechua (Andean), and Danish. Can your listeners pick out a word they like and write it?

SUGGESTED READINGS

Beaty, J. J., & Pratt, L. (2011). *Early literacy in preschool and kindergarten: A multicultural perspective.* 3rd ed. Boston: Pearson.

Kirk, E. W., & Clark, P. (2005). Beginning with names: Using children's names to facilitate early literacy learning. *Childhood Education, 81*(3), 139–144.

Schickedanz, J. A., & Casbergue, R. M. (2009). *Writing in preschool: Learning to orchestrate meaning and marks,* 2nd ed. Newark, DE: International Reading Association.

Temple, C. A., Nathan, R. G., & Burris, N. A. (1993). *The beginnings of writing.* Boston: Allyn & Bacon.

Taking Dictation

CONCEPT

Tunks and Giles (2009) tell us: "Adults take dictation when they listen to and write down children's oral stories before the children can write on their own" (p. 22). Why should this be important in children's learning to write and read? For one thing, it helps children see that certain speech sounds can be connected to specific letters. As Schickedanz and Casbergue (2009) note, many young children can recognize and name all the letters of the alphabet but have no idea how to use them to make words (p. 50).

When teachers say aloud the children's words they are writing down, children begin to understand what writing is all about. Taking dictation on the part of the teacher has other benefits:

1. It introduces children to the purpose of writing and the function of the printed language.

2. Children become aware of the speech-to-text connection as they watch the words they speak take shape on paper or white board.

3. They begin to understand that what they say can be written down and then read back—their words are permanent!

4. Children gain ownership of their own stories.

Is there a best time to take children's dictations? Some teachers like to start off the day by taking dictation when children come to school in the morning with experiences to share. Large- or small-group discussions are another opportunity for children to dictate their stories. Other opportunities for dictation include after field trips, in learning centers when an activity is completed, and after science experiments. Sometimes when children enjoy a particular book they want to extend the story by adding their own narrative. When children are compiling their autobiographies or doing journal writing teachers are often called upon to take dictation until the children have developed their own writing skills.

Is there a best way to for teachers to take dictation? Figure 21–1 lists some ideas. Most important is having children sit close enough to see what the teacher is writing. If they pay close enough attention they will come to understand that each word they say is being recorded on the paper. If you say the words aloud as you write them, the children come to understand the concept that spoken words can be written.

Children dictate their story as the teacher writes it down.

> - Write children's words just as they are spoken.
> - Track print with a finger or pointer as you write.
> - Write legibly.
> - Use standard spelling.
> - Have children sit where they can watch.
> - Read dictation back to children.
> - Track print as you read.

FIGURE 21–1   How to Take Children's Dictations.

Activities

Help children become deeply involved in one of the topics you are pursuing—for example, making collections.

1. Making collections. The children in one class had fun making collections during their science projects. One collection was stones of different colors. Another child brought in her collection of seashells from a beach she had visited. The teacher asked if they would like to have stories about their collections written down. They would. Children in each small group dictated the information about one of their collections while the teacher wrote it down.

To get them started the teacher read the rhyming story of ***Zachary Z. Packrat and His Amazing Collections*** (Bessesen, B., 2008, Phoenix, AZ: Arizona Highways Book Division). This cartoon packrat tells a long humorous story of the dozens of knickknacks, tidbits, relics, mementos, and doodads he finds and stores in his bungalow. Just like his human counterparts, Zack meets friends every Saturday mornings for a swap meet of rare relics and unique antiques. Children love to laugh over his wacky collection, and can't wait to tell the reader about their own trips with their parents to swap meets and flea markets. Give each child a chance to dictate his story while you write it where the storyteller can see the words.

SUGGESTED READINGS

Lindfors, J. W. (2008). *Children's language: Connecting reading, writing, and talk.* New York: Teachers College Press.

Schickedanz, J. A., & Casbergue, R. M. (2009). *Writing in preschool: Learning to orchestrate meaning and marks,* 2nd ed. Newark, DE: International Reading Association.

Tunks, K. W., & Giles, R. M. (2009). Writing their words: Strategies for supporting young authors. *Young Children, 64*(1), 22–25.

Caption Pictures

22

CONCEPT

Children's first story writing often takes the form of pictures that they draw or paint about something they have done or something that has happened to them. The story may be one initiated by the teacher who suggests they draw a picture of a field trip they have taken or a science project they have worked on. On the other hand, it may originate with a child who wants to draw a picture in her journal of something that happened to her. When children ask the teacher to write their story on their picture, usually at the top or bottom, we call these drawings *caption pictures.*

For most children the caption will be dictated by them to be written by the teacher. As children become more experienced drawing caption pictures, creating stories for them, and hearing the stories read aloud, some will make their own scribble-writing captions under their pictures. Others will be able to collaborate with the teacher and begin to write their own captions.

What can children learn from their caption pictures? Teachers who involve children in this kind of drawing say that caption pictures help children to:

- Make a connection between spoken and written language
- See how their spoken language is written down.
- See what words look like that are used to label objects in their pictures.
- See how the words they spoke are spelled.
- See how a story is written.
- Develop a "sense of story."
- Begin to write their own captions/stories.

Activities

*1. Read **I Really, Really Need Actual Ice Skates*** (Child, L., 2009, New York: Dial Books). The children in one class loved the Charlie and Lola stories and couldn't wait for a new one. The ice-skating book quickly became one of the children's favorites. They were soon acting out this rather complex story of Lola, who started out wanting a scooter but then changed her mind when the children's friends Marv and Morten took them ice skating. But when Lola fell on the ice and Morten fell off his scooter, Lola didn't want ice skates anymore. It was too *wobble-ob-erley.* Would their dads let Morten and Lola trade? Yes. But then as Lola scootered along, she saw Evie going *boing, boing* on her pogo stick. "Oh, that looks fun . . ."

The teacher invited these 4- and 5-year-olds to make their own books about their favorite outdoor sports. All of the children who drew pictures dictated picture captions to the teacher, who wrote them down. From this experience, the teacher learned that:

- Favorite sports made an excellent topic for children to draw and write about (see Figure 22–1).
- Using a favorite book as a lead-in was especially successful.
- Listening to children's picture captions and following their lead could result in valuable new literacy experiences.
- Starting with one particular picture could lead to the creation of an entire book with a plot and characters. (See Figure 22–2.)
- Caption pictures can help teachers discover which children have developed a "sense of story."

FIGURE 22–1 That's a healthy apple and strawberry that helps me to roller skate.

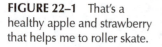

FIGURE 22–2 Me and RJ the racoon eating pancakes and having a tea party outside under the big umbrella watching our friend Mariah playing hopscotch.

2. Start with a picture. In this case, the teacher decided to start with the picture that most resembled an ongoing story. (See Figure 22–2.) She asked the child artist if she wanted to make a whole book. The girl agreed. The teacher asked the girl: "What happens next?"

> *Girl: Mariah wants to come to our tea party, but RJ Raccoon doesn't want her to.*
>
> *Teacher: What does she do? Can you draw a picture about that?*

Once the girl had drawn the picture and dictated the caption, the teacher continued, asking her, "And then what happens?" When the story was completed, the teacher wrote captions on the pictures, just as the girl dictated them, and stapled the book together along with a cover the girl made. The book was placed in the book center for everyone to read.

*3. Read **Bounce*** (Cronin, D., 2007, New York: Atheneum). For children who like simpler stories, read the rhyming story **Bounce,** about a jumping dog who leads the listeners to hip hop like a bunny,

FIGURE 22–3 Children playing soccer under an apple tree.

FIGURE 22–4 I jump on my trampoline.

bounce a volley ball, a soccer ball, and a beach ball, then try to bounce on roller skates (no), and on a pogo stick (yes). One child drew three children playing soccer. (See Figure 22–3.) A boy drew his own experience of bouncing on his trampoline. (See Figure 22–4.)

4. Say the words aloud as you write the caption. It is important for you to repeat the words the child dictates as you write them on the picture. Read the sentence aloud after it is completed (Neuman & Roskos, 1993, p. 214). This helps the child to see how spoken language is written. Then ask the child if he would like to read the sentence. Run your finger under the words as he reads.

SUGGESTED READINGS

Baghban, M. (2007). Scribbles, labels, and stories: The role of drawing in the development of writing. *Young Children, 62*(1), 20–26.

Neuman, S. B., & Roskos, K. A. (1993). *Language and literacy learning in the early years: An integrated approach.* Fort Worth, TX: Harcourt.

Soundy, C. S., Guha, S., & Qui, Y. (2007). Picture power: Placing artistry and literacy on the same page. *Young Children, 62*(3), 82–88.

Easel Painting

23

CONCEPT

Some teachers may wonder why painting is included as a literacy strategy. Yet many aspects of child development overlap. Thus many activities that help children to develop serve several purposes. Easel painting, for example, is a highly creative pursuit. It helps children develop artistic skills and at the same time helps them to develop certain literacy skills, as shown in Figure 23–1. For young children, art is a natural language. They emerge into painting/drawing just as they do into writing: first scribbles, then shapes, and finally pictures/letters. Easel painting is especially important for this emergence to take place because it involves the *freedom* for young children to explore and experiment on their own with the paint medium.

In the beginning children play around with brush and paint, trying to figure out which hand to use, how to hold the brush, and how to dip the brush into the paint and spread it onto the paper without dripping it all over. Their first attempts are splashes across the paper. Then as they gain control, they begin scribbling different colors on the paper, often one on top of the other, sometimes using one hand and then the other. They are not painting a picture but working through the process of learning how to paint. Once again they are progressing through the three spontaneous steps of self-discovery: *manipulation, mastery,* and *meaning.* (See Strategy 19, "Alphabet.") Once they have learned how to manipulate this unfamiliar medium, they go on to their own self-imposed mastery by painting the

This child has painted an interesting picture she may want to talk about.

> • Finger strength to hold a writing implement
> • Eye-hand coordination to make shapes and letters
> • Practice in making letter shapes
> • Knowledge that their pictures can communicate

FIGURE 23–1   Literacy Skills from Easel Painting.

same thing over and over. For some children it is merely one scribble in the center of a sheet, then the same thing on another sheet—again and again. Do not interfere. They are not "wasting paper," but practicing their newfound skill.

Eventually they progress to making scribble pictures that they may name before, during, or after they paint them. These too evolve through certain stages, as illustrated in Figure 23–2. By now, some youngsters are also making lines of scribble writing above or below their pictures to tell the story of what they have painted. (See Strategy 22, "Caption Pictures.") They are beginning to differentiate between scribble writing and scribble painting. Others have stumbled onto making alphabet letters with their paintbrush.

Thus, teachers need to be aware that easel painting can also serve as easel writing. As adults, we need to examine what words mean to us. If we think easel "painting" is for painting pictures only, we may miss altogether the "writing" many young children do at the easel. As Baghban (2007) says, "The frequent predominance of drawing in development is important because drawing promotes the first writing, and this writing becomes the first reading material that children themselves author" (p. 22).

The same concept holds true for finger painting. For some children, finger painting can also be "finger printing" or "finger writing." (See Strategy 24, "Finger Painting.") As with easel painting, it is often the teacher who makes the distinction by pointing out to the child that he has made a letter: "Look, Paul. You have painted the letter 'b.' Can you find any other letters in your painting?"

Activities

1. Observe scribble painting to see if children are making letters. Observe children's scribble painting carefully to see if they are attempting to scribble write with their paint. If you see a real or mock letter within their scribble painting, point it out to the youngsters and see what other letters they can find or make. Can they do it again? Sometimes children are purposely trying to paint a letter, but often letters happen only by accident.

2. Have children scribble paint their names at the bottom of their pictures. Once children evolve from the scribble stage of easel painting into the pictorial stage, painted letters usually appear only in their names at the bottom of the paper. Some children do paint a line of real or pretend writing under their pictures to tell the story. Others ask the teacher to write what they want to say about it. By now they can sign their names, even if only in scribbles.

3. Set up easels ahead of time. Set up easels ahead of time with two or three jars of liquid tempera paint and chubby brushes. Fasten large sheets of white paper to each side of the easel. Young children need room to try out large motions with their brushes. Small sheets of copy paper are too confining. Hang as many painting aprons nearby as there are spaces to paint. As with computer chairs, it is best to have two stand-up easels next to one another so children can check on each other's work and converse about what they are doing.

4. Encourage children to talk about their paintings. Help the children use painting as a scaffold for their early writing efforts. Teachers who observe children's progress over time as they paint, listen to their words, and engage them in conversations can often tell whether they are exploring the medium, trying to master it, or trying to represent something. If they have expressed an intent to represent something, you have an opening to talk with children about their pictures as they paint.

You must do it carefully. Asking "What is it?" can be an insult, when to the child it is perfectly obvious that he is painting his house. Commenting "What a beautiful picture!" does not even call for a response. Saying "Tell me about your picture" may not elicit much information either, because the child may not know what to say. Oken-Wright (1998) encourages teachers to ask instead: "What's happening here?" and indicate a specific part of the picture. This may begin a dialogue that turns into a story narrative, with the child adding to the story as she paints (p. 78).

FIGURE 23–2 Stages of Art Development.
Source: From *Skills for preschool teachers* by J. Beaty, 1996, Upper Saddle River, NJ: Merrill/ Prentice Hall. Reprinted with permission of B. Helm.

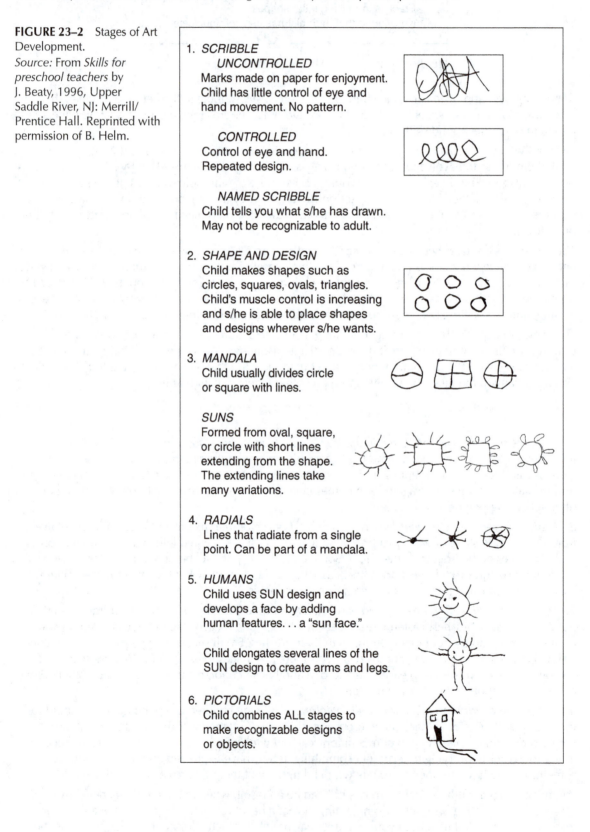

1. *SCRIBBLE*
   UNCONTROLLED
   Marks made on paper for enjoyment. Child has little control of eye and hand movement. No pattern.

   CONTROLLED
   Control of eye and hand. Repeated design.

   NAMED SCRIBBLE
   Child tells you what s/he has drawn. May not be recognizable to adult.

2. *SHAPE AND DESIGN*
   Child makes shapes such as circles, squares, ovals, triangles. Child's muscle control is increasing and s/he is able to place shapes and designs wherever s/he wants.

3. *MANDALA*
   Child usually divides circle or square with lines.

   SUNS
   Formed from oval, square, or circle with short lines extending from the shape. The extending lines take many variations.

4. *RADIALS*
   Lines that radiate from a single point. Can be part of a mandala.

5. *HUMANS*
   Child uses SUN design and develops a face by adding human features. . . a "sun face."

   Child elongates several lines of the SUN design to create arms and legs.

6. *PICTORIALS*
   Child combines ALL stages to make recognizable designs or objects.

ADVANTAGES OF EASEL PAINTING

One of the big advantages of easel painting is that the easels are always there, ready to be used. By standing upright, they beckon to children to come and paint. Some teachers prefer to have children do flat painting with the easel paper laid out on tables or the floor. Although this is perfectly acceptable, easels are still more convenient for everyone involved, and a reminder to children that it's always time to paint.

SUGGESTED READINGS

Baghban, M. (2007). Scribbles, labels, and stories: The role of drawing in the development of writing. *Young Children, 62*(1), 20–26.

Cherry, C. (1972). *Creative art for the developing child.* Belmont, CA: Fearon.

Dyson, A. H. (1988). Appreciate the drawing and dictating of young children. *Young Children, 43*(3), 25–32.

Kane, F. (1982). Thinking, drawing—Writing, reading. *Childhood Education, 58*(May–June), 292–299.

Kellogg, R. (1970). *Analyzing children's art.* Palo Alto, CA: National Press Books.

Oken-Wright, P. (1998). Transition to writing: Drawing as a scaffold for emergent writers. *Young Children, 53*(2), 76–81.

Finger Painting

CONCEPT

Like easel painting, finger painting also encourages children to write as well as draw. Finger painting consists of spreading paint on paper placed on a table or floor, or directly on a desktop or tray. A child then moves the paint around with his fingers, hand, arm, or a stick, making swirls, designs, or sometimes letters. The finished results on paper can be dried and displayed. Finger painting on a desktop or tray can be recovered by placing blank paper over it and rubbing until the paint and design adhere to the paper.

Children enjoy finger painting because it is so easy to make a mark, rub it out, and start all over. No need to pick up a brush or tool. A swipe of the hand can create a design. Another swipe can wipe it out. Experimenting with this flowing hand and finger movement gives children freedom to create an unlimited variety of forms. Some children do hand stamping in the paint. Others draw intricate designs with one finger. Those trying to master the medium may make the same swirls over and over.

A few stumble onto scribble writing and letter printing almost by accident. As Temple, Nathan, and Burris (1993) remind us, "Learning to write is largely an act of discovery" (p. 2). Once they realize they can make letters in their finger paint, some children begin making them over and over, as well. Teachers may point out such letters to the children. On the other hand, most children do not differentiate writing from drawing in the beginning.

Activities

1. Set up finger painting. Wet the paper (finger paint paper, butcher paper, or shelf lining paper are best) and place it on a smooth flat surface. One scoop of one tempera color paint can be heaped in the middle of the paper ready to be smeared around by the painter. Have a container of the paint and a scoop nearby so children can add more when necessary. Once children have become used to this sort of painting, put out two colors of paint and let them mix the colors as they paint. Because finger painting is messy, you will also need to provide painting aprons, a bucket of water, and paper towels nearby.

2. Use a variety of painting materials. Tempera paint is usually the medium of choice for finger painting, but there are other possibilities. Children enjoy variety. Once they are used to doing finger painting in tempera paint, try something different. For instance, liquid starch, liquid soap, or white paste can be used. Color the new medium with tempera paint or food coloring. Squirting shaving cream on a tabletop also offers a fine finger painting experience. Tabletop painting gives the child more freedom since she is not limited to the size of the paper.

Another possible medium (and it is free) is mud. Children love to play in mud and should welcome the opportunity to finger paint in mud. Bring in a bucket from outside and add some liquid soap or liquid starch for transparency.

3. Encourage writing in the paint. Once a child has finished her painting, ask her to sign her name at the bottom. Children who have not learned how can scribble write their names. Read a simple story with a favorite character to a small group of children before the finger painting activity. Afterwards, ask them to draw a picture of the character. Accept whatever they draw, even scribbles. Be sure they sign their names. Stories you could read might include those shown in Figure 24–1.

Children can also be encouraged to write notes or letters, or make up their own stories in finger paint. These can be dried and mounted for their authors to "read" to the class afterwards.

81

Bats at the Beach, Lies, B., 2006

Captain Cheech, Marin, C., 2008

Doctor Ted, Beaty, A., 2008

Duck on a Bike, Shannon, D., 2002

Grumpy Gloria, Dewdney, A., 2006

I Love Bugs, Dodd, E., 2010

I'm Your Bus, Singer, M., 2009

The Little Red Pen, Stevens, J., 2011

Owl Babies, Waddell, M., 1992

FIGURE 24–1 Character Stories for Finger Painting.

SUGGESTED READINGS

Beaty, J. J., & Pratt, L. (2011). *Early literacy in preschool and kindergarten: A multicultural perspective.* 3rd ed. Boston: Pearson.

Edwards, L. C. (2006). *The creative arts: A process approach for teachers and children.* 3rd ed. Upper Saddle River, NJ: Merrill/Prentice Hall.

Temple, C. A., Nathan, R. G., & Burris, N. A. (1993). *The beginnings of writing.* Boston: Allyn & Bacon.

Chalk

CONCEPT

Chalk

Drawing implements such as chalk can also become writing implements when the time is right. Young children emerge into writing through experimenting with all sorts of tools: paintbrushes, pencils, pens, markers, chalk, crayons, sticks, and even their fingers. But even before they use chalk for writing, many young children begin to draw pictures with it. Often they are drawing to tell a story, still another way chalk can lead children into literacy.

It is important not to push children into representational drawing before they have satisfied their drive to explore the medium (Oken-Wright, 1998). First of all they need to learn on their own how chalk works. When young children first pick up a piece of chalk (make sure it is a thick one), they tend to play with it, moving it lightly or scribbling it firmly all over a chalkboard, the sidewalk, or the paper you provide. They are engaged in the *manipulation* level of self-discovery play. They need to work their way through this initial experimentation before you can expect them to draw a picture or write a letter.

You will know when they have finally "got the hang of it" when they repeat the same scribbles or designs over and over. They have progressed to the self-imposed practice level we call *mastery*. Finally,

Children draw scribbles and shapes on chalkboards before they make letters.

they arrive at *meaning* when they begin to put meaning into their drawings. (See Strategy 19, "Alphabet.") If you push children to draw what you want them to draw, or ask them to tell you what they have drawn, you may short-circuit their self-exploratory play and discourage them from continuing.

Drawing eventually leads to talking and writing, so be sure to give children plenty of time to explore the medium of chalk before you ask them to talk. If you observe what children are doing with chalk from day to day, you should be able to determine how they are progressing through the levels of manipulation, mastery, and meaning.

Activities

1. Grocery bag drawing. Start with a small group of children, no more than five or six. Give them each a thick piece of white chalk and a large brown grocery bag, brown wrapping paper, or a place at the chalkboard if you have one. Also provide each of the children with an eraser or sponge for erasing their work. Have them "experiment with their chalk" to see what it does and what they can do with it.

2. Paper roll drawing on floor. Some will want more paper when theirs gets "too messed up." You may want to start with a large roll of brown wrapping paper that you unroll across the floor if you have no chalkboard. Children love to work on the floor. Make sure there is plenty of room for everyone in the group. Bring in a CD player or cassette recorder and put in music that will play softly as they work.

3. Talking about drawings. Choose your own comments about the children's chalk drawings carefully. To ask them "What is it?" is not appropriate, for they will be engaged in a process, not a picture. Even comments such as "Tell me about your drawing" may not elicit a real answer because there is nothing to tell, or they may make up something just to please you. Better to use words of encouragement such as "I like the way you're holding the chalk today, Heather," or "You certainly worked hard with your chalk today, Keshawn," or "You filled the whole paper today, Amber. Good for you." Oken-Wright (1998) suggests that a better open-ended question for eliciting a response may be: "What's happening here?" (p. 78).

4. Listening to children's comments. Eventually some of the children may want to talk about what they are drawing because they have progressed to the meaning level in their exploration. Listen to what they are saying to each other as they draw. Some children may declare their intention of what they plan to draw before they start. Others pick up their ideas from one another and talk about their drawings as they work on them. Still others may be willing to talk about their drawings to the group when they are finished.

5. Working in small groups. Working in small groups like this, where everyone sees what the others are doing and shares ideas, helps the entire group to progress in drawing and talking skills. Because chalk is a temporary medium that can be erased easily, even the shyest child will be encouraged to try it.

6. Chalk storytelling. Now you can start your "chalk talking" sessions on a daily basis. Does anyone have a story to tell about his drawing? This can be the beginning of children's storytelling in your class, an important precursor to story reading for children.

Yolanda stands at the chalkboard and draws her story as she tells it. She talks about her family, telling about her mother, father, brothers and sisters, the new baby, and her gerbil. You can make an audio recording of Yolanda's story, if she agrees, and transcribe it for her in the book she is making, where she can illustrate it again with colored chalk, markers, or crayons. (See Strategy 26, "Shared Writing.")

7. Sidewalk drawing. If your children enjoy drawing with chalk, there are several other chalk experiences they should try. *Sidewalk chalk* can be used outside on a sidewalk or driveway, but be sure to get permission first. Many children like to squat down to draw with thick pieces of white or colored sidewalk chalk on a surface that is much grainier than chalkboards or paper. Their drawings tend to spread out across the walk. They may or may not want to talk about them.

But if you "read" them the book **Chalk** (Thomson, B., 2010, Tarrytown, NY: Marshall Cavendish), a ferocious story may emerge about three children who go out to the playground on a rainy day and find a bag of sidewalk chalk dangling from the jaws of a dinosaur climber. This is a wordless story, so the children will have to make up their own words. They can dictate about the girl who draws a yellow sun on the sidewalk, which causes the real sun to come out and dry up all the rain; about a second girl who draws orange butterflies that come to life and fill the sky; and finally about the boy who draws a green dinosaur that comes to life and . . . Have them guess how the story ends before you turn the pages. Then give them sidewalk chalk to draw their own exciting stories.

8. *Wet paper or wet chalk drawing.* To keep colored chalk drawings from rubbing off the paper, sheets of high-quality paper can be moistened with a sponge before children draw on them, or liquid starch can be sponged on the paper to keep it moist and provide a better finish. Instead of wetting the paper, the colored chalk itself can be soaked in a solution of sugar water (1/3 cup of sugar to 1 cup water) for five minutes before use to increase the brilliance of the colors. As the chalk dries out, it can be dipped in the sugar water.

9. *Chalk writing.* Most initial scribbling that young children do with chalk eventually turns into representational drawing, as previously mentioned. But some of the scribbles can also become early writing. Children often recognize that teachers write words under their pictures, so they pretend to do the same with horizontal scribble writing.

SUGGESTED READINGS

Beaty, J. J., & Pratt, L. (2011). *Early literacy in preschool and kindergarten: A multicultural perspective.* 3rd ed. Boston: Pearson.

Healy, L. I. (2001). Applying theory to practice: Using developmentally appropriate strategies to help children draw. *Young Children, 56*(4), 28–30.

Oken-Wright, P. (1998). Transition to writing: Drawing as a scaffold for emergent writers. *Young Children, 53*(2), 76–81.

Shared Writing

CONCEPT

Shared writing is an emergent literacy concept in which children dictate a story and the teacher writes it down. Then the teacher reads the story back to the child and encourages the child to read it aloud herself while it is fresh in her mind. Sometimes called the "language experience approach," this strategy is often a favorite for both teachers and children. Vukelich and Christie (2009) tell us that shared writing is an excellent way to demonstrate the relationship between oral and written language: "It helps children to realize that what they say can be written down in print and that print can be read back as oral language" (p. 5).

As the teacher writes the story on chart paper or a chalkboard, the child or small group of children can see how words that are spoken can be turned into print. They watch the teacher write the words from left to right in a line and from top to bottom on the sheet or board. She starts the sentences with a capital letter and ends them with a period. They also see how she spells the words and leave spaces between them. Thus they are able to get a clear picture of how the mechanics of writing work.

This does not mean they will be required to produce such conventional writing. After all, some are still at the scribble-writing stage. But shared stories like this can be a model for all kinds of writing and reading. Chart sheets of children's oral stories can be saved and reread from time to time just like books in the book center. If teachers repeat the reading of these stories enough, children will be able to follow along and read the stories themselves. Just like with shared reading, the teacher can read part of a sentence and pause for a child to finish it. She should remember what comes next if the story was from her own experience. Run your finger slowly under the words as you say them. Then stop so the listener can fill in what comes next. Figure 21–1 gives suggestions on how the teacher should take children's dictations.

Activities

1. Have children tell their own stories. When something unusual or exciting happens to a child ask him or her to tell it into a tape recorder or dictate it to the teacher as she writes it down. Try to use the children's own words. At first you may need to prompt them in the rereading of the story. But they will find it much easier to reread such a story if it is their own, with their own words.

2. Use caption pictures to stimulate story writing. (See Strategy 22, "Caption Pictures.") When children's drawings motivate an entire story and not just a brief caption, you can write the story on chart paper one sentence at a time. Say the words aloud as the child dictates them. Then reread each sentence aloud after it is completed. This helps the child to see how spoken language is written. Then ask the child if he would like to read the sentence. Run your finger under the words as he reads.

One child told a story about going camping and sitting around a campfire. The class was talking about eating good foods to make you healthy and wondered how going camping did that. He made a drawing to show how (see Figure 26–1), which prompted the teacher to ask if he would like to make a book about going camping. He did. The teacher wrote what he dictated on chart paper. Then she printed out the story on the computer and had the child help staple it together along with the picture into a book.

FIGURE 26–1 Eat fruit and vegetables by the campfire so you can win lifting weights.

FIGURE 26–2 A big sister and a little sister swinging. They got off the swings when their mom called them to eat some blueberries, strawberries, and carrots.

Another child told about how swinging in her backyard helped her and her sister stay healthy. She wanted their picture and story included in the camping book. (See Figure 26–2.) This was just the beginning of the book "How We Stay Healthy."

SUGGESTED READINGS

Baghban, M. (2007). Scribbles, labels, and stories: The role of drawing in the development of writing. *Young Children, 62*(1), 20–26.

Soundy, C. S., Guha, S., & Qui, Y. (2007). Picture power: Placing artistry and literacy on the same page. *Young Children, 62*(3), 82–88.

Strickland, D. S., & Schickedanz, J. S. (2009). *Learning about print in preschool: Working with letters, words, and beginning links with phonemic awareness.* 2nd ed. Newark, DE: International Reading Association.

Vukelich, C., & Christie, J. (2009). *Building a foundation for preschool literacy: Effective instruction for children's reading and writing development.* 2nd ed. Newark, DE: International Reading Association.

27 Dual Language Learners' Writing

CONCEPT

Just as English-speaking children emerge into writing by *discovering* how it works, dual language learners (bilingual learners) learn to write in both their home language and English through discovery. As Shagoury (2009a) notes, "Young dual language learners actively figure out the way written language works in their first and second language" (p. 53). Once they are aware of written language at home and in school they actively engage in trying it out for themselves. As pioneer language specialist Emilia Ferreiro (1980) tells us, "Children have shown us that they need to reconstruct the written system in order to make it their own" (p. 56).

For instance, the writing scribbles of an Arabic child may contain many dots and squiggles as he emerges into writing both English and Arabic. (See *The Day of Ahmed's Secret*, Lewin, T., 1990, New York: Lothrup, Lee, & Shepard.) The writing scribbles of a Chinese child may show characteristics of Chinese characters. (See *The Pet Dragon*, Nieman, C., 2008, New York: Greenwillow.) Both may also make shapes that represent the English alphabet that they see around them. Teachers are often surprised to learn that dual language learners can learn to write before mastering a spoken second language and also that children who learn literacy in their home language do not need to relearn these skills in school. They transfer this learning to their second language (Ferreiro, 1980, p. 55).

Preschool programs that allow and encourage dual language children to develop their home language to high levels are more successful than English-only programs, according to Shin (2010). Figure 27–1 includes suggestions for helping dual language learners emerge into writing.

Activities

1. Read the bilingual book **Bebé Goes Shopping** (Elya, S., 2006, Orlando, FL: Harcourt). Here is a peppy, colorful book about Mom (*mama*) taking Baby (*bebe*) with her as she pushes a shopping cart (*carrito*) through a large supermarket (*supermercado*). The story is in English, but Spanish words are inserted in sentences here and there. Baby tries to grab different packages off the shelves, but Mom tries to distract him by giving him her keys (*llaves*). Finally a package of animal crackers calms him down.

Read to two children at a time so they can see the action along with the Spanish words in boldface type. Afterwards have the listeners tell you what Mom bought as you write the words in English and Spanish. Maybe they would like to make their own shopping list in either language.

FIGURE 27–1 Helping Dual Language Learners to Write.

- Do not force children to write; make it fun.
- Include in shared writing some words in a different language.
- Ask what an object is called in a home language.
- Write it down in the home language and English.
- Clap syllables of words in children's home languages.
- Have alphabet books in different languages.
- Give children time to repeat activities over and over.

FIGURE 27–2 I love carrots ["zanahoria"] because they make me happy.

*2. Read **Gathering the Sun: An Alphabet in Spanish and English*** (Ada, A., 1997, New York: Lothrop, Lee, & Shepard). Each radiant full-color spread shows Mexican workers harvesting a different crop. A brief verse in Spanish and in English is inserted on every page. Make a list containing English and Spanish words of the vegetables, fruit, and people illustrated. Go over the list with your listeners. Can they choose their favorites and draw a picture of them? (See Figure 27–2.)

SUGGESTED READINGS

Ferreiro, E. (1980). The relationship between oral and written language: The children's viewpoints. In M. Haussler, D. Strickland, & Y. Goodman (Eds.), *Oral and written language development research: Impact on schools* (pp. 47–56). Urbana, IL: International Reading Association.

Nemeth, K. N. (2009). *Many languages, one classroom: Teaching dual and English language learners.* Beltsville, MD: Gryphon House.

Shagoury, R. (2009a). Language to language: Nurturing writing development in multilingual classrooms. *Young Children, 64*(2), 52–57.

Shagoury, R. E. (2009b). *Raising writers: Understanding and nurturing young children's writing development.* Boston: Pearson.

Shin, S. J. (2010). Teaching English language learners: Recommendations of early childhood educators. *Dimensions of Early Childhood, 38*(2), 13–20.

Strickland, D. S., & Schickedanz, J. A. (2009). *Learning about print in preschool: Working with letters, words, and beginning links with phonemic awareness.* 2nd ed. Newark, DE: International Reading Association.

 # Invented Spelling

CONCEPT

As children see and interact with the environmental print around them in the classroom (e.g., signs, job charts, attendance charts, recipe charts, labels on the aquarium, and labels in each of the learning centers), some, but not all of them, will begin to internalize ideas about written words.

Some youngsters will realize, just as they did when they first learned to talk, that everything has a name and that this name can be written. If you have set up your classroom with a writing center and writing materials, these children may begin experimenting with writing words. These words may be scribbles or letter strings at first. (See Strategy 16, "Emergent Writing.") As children become more familiar with letters and their sounds, they may start putting letters together to make words. Not all preschool children will arrive at this point.

Writing their first words should be as exciting as speaking their first words. But some adults are disappointed because the children have not spelled the words correctly. Why should they? Spelling has little to do with children's writing their first words, just as correct pronunciation has little to do with children's speaking their first words. They are trying the best they know how. Proper spelling will come later, not through your corrections, but with experience and refinement.

We used to think that spelling was a rote skill, depending on memorization. Shagoury (2009) now tells us: "Current research has shown that, like learning to talk, learning to spell is a language function. Both depend on invention, interaction, and risk-taking" (p. 53). Some young children put letters together that sound like the word. First words are often made up mostly of consonants: *skwl* for *school; das* for *days*. Some literacy specialists call this *invented spelling*. Others call it *phonemic spelling* because the children are beginning to understand the connection between sounds (phonemes) and letters (Schickedanz & Casbergue, 2009). Children are actually *emerging into literacy* right before your eyes. Do not correct them. Encourage them to do all the writing they can. Have them read their words aloud. Challenge them to write a message to a friend, to their parent, to you. Be sure to answer them with your own note. With experience and maturity they will eventually change from invented spelling to conventional spelling on their own—just as they changed from baby talk to conventional speech on their own.

For young children to write words in the first place indicates that they have developed what Opitz (2000, p. 6) calls *phonological awareness* or sound awareness. This awareness comes from hearing words being spoken. But to write words, children must also become aware of certain concepts regarding writing. If children are still writing strings of letters, you will know they have not yet developed this phonological awareness, as defined in Figure 28–1.

FIGURE 28–1
Phonological Awareness.

- Written words name things.
- Written words convey messages that can be read.
- Words are made up of certain letters.
- The letters in the word say the sound of the word.
- Words represent a sound unit (word awareness).
- Words are made up of different parts (syllables).
- Words are made up of different sounds (phonemes).

Children who use invented spelling have progressed a step beyond this letter-string stage. Their spelling indicates they are phonemically aware; that is, they know what letters represent the sounds of the words they are writing. They may not be spelling the words conventionally because they do not know how yet, but they are exhibiting an exciting breakthrough on the road to emergent literacy. They are spelling words "phonetically." Your job is to support them in this new understanding by providing them with time, writing materials, and opportunities to use their newfound skill. They are experimenting with writing (manipulating the medium) just as they do with any new thing. Having them write on lined paper is not helpful. Young children's experiments with letters and words just do not fit on a line.

What about printing out words correctly for children to copy, you may ask? No. Then they would not be extracting their own rules about how writing works. You must be careful not to take over the writing process from young children at this point. For emergent writing to occur, children must maintain control of the process themselves (Schrader & Hoffman, 1987, p. 11).

Activities

1. Label photos. Have each child in a small group in the writing center choose one of the photos you have put out about classroom activities. Have them paste the photo onto a blank sheet of unlined paper. Talk to each one about the photo and how they would label it (e.g., "ETSaBKHS" for "It's a block house"). Accept whatever they write, even scribbles.

2. Label children's photos. Put out photos of each child in a small group. Have them paste the photo onto a sheet of paper and have them write: "My name is _____" under the photo ("MI NM S JeremY"). Accept whatever they write.

3. Caption pictures. Ask children who are painting at an easel or at a table to write something about their easel picture. Scribbles are acceptable. (For example. "ETS Me N MI DG" might be a scribbled form of "It's me and my dog.")

*4. Read **Wallace's Lists*** (Bottner, B., & Kruglik, G., 2004, New York: Katherine Tegen Books). This book is about Wallace who has to have a "to do" list about everything in his life, until he meets a new neighbor who shows him how to live without a list. Children who are beginning to write words enjoy making lists. Have them pretend to be Wallace and make a list of foods they like to eat or games they like to play, writing and spelling words as best they can.

SUGGESTED READINGS

Opitz, M. F. (2000). *Rhymes & reasons: Literature and language play for phonological awareness.* Portsmouth, NH: Heinemann.

Sansome, R. M. (1988). SKWL DAS: Emerging literacy in children. *Day Care and Early Education, 16*(1), 14–19.

Schickedanz, J. A., & Casbergue, R. M. (2009). *Writing in preschool: Learning to orchestrate meaning and marks.* 2nd Ed. Newark, DE: International Reading Association.

Schrader, C. T., & Hoffman, S. (1987). Encouraging children's early writing efforts. *Day Care and Early Education, 15*(2), 9–13.

Shagoury, R. E. (2009). *Raising writers: Understanding and nurturing young children's writing development.* Boston: Pearson.

Journals, Literature Logs

CONCEPT

As preschool children begin honing their scribble-writing skills along with their drawing ability, teachers need to set up activities that encourage them to practice these skills. Drawing and writing in a journal every day is a favorite method because it combines these abilities in an authentic situation. Children are able to make an actual record of things that happen to them daily. Not only do children get to practice their writing/scribbling, but the journals they produce give the teacher an overview of their progress.

When children do their own drawings and writing/scribbling about picture books they are hearing read to them, the records they keep are called *literature logs*. As with daily journals, these logs are also kept over a period of time and are generally based on a particular theme (Soundy, Guha, & Qui, 2007, p. 86). They are not actual happenings as in children's daily journals, but are usually about books being read or imaginary trips being taken.

Journal writing has long been a practice in elementary schools, but journaling with preschool youngsters may be a new experience in many programs. The focus on early literacy now begins in preschool. Young children's emergent writing experiences include notes, messages, signs, lists, letters, and stories that have now become an accepted part of the curriculum.

You may wonder: How can children who do not already write be expected to keep a journal? Children learn to write by writing. They see writing produced around them in the form of environmental print, attendance charts, recipe charts, the daily schedule, lists, and stories the teacher records on newsprint. Now it is their turn to record their own doings. They do not hesitate. Even children who cannot write their own names happily fill their journal pages with scribbles that represent pictures and words.

Teachers staple together five sheets of unlined paper, one for every day of the week, and put them into each child's cubby or mailbox on Monday. Staff members work with individuals or small groups of children to get them started, then talk with them daily about their work in positive terms. Some children draw pictures only. Others make lines of scribbles. Some do both. A few write words.

Literature logs, using the same five sheets of stapled-together paper, can be completed by children after a science project, a field trip, or some other theme-based activity that is tied in with picture books.

Activities

*1. Read **Diary of a Worm** (Cronin, D., 2003, New York: Joanna Cotler Books).* This fanciful tale has the date at the top of the page and a simple text under the pictures telling something the worm did that day. For instance, on March 29, the worm tells how he tried to teach spider how to dig. After reading this story to a small group, go back to one of the days and write the date at the top of a newsprint pad. Ask your listeners what they would record for this day if they were the worm. You can record what they tell you. Then give them each a blank page labeled March 29 and have them record whatever they think the worm would write/draw. Help them get started. Scribbles are okay.

*2. Read **Diary of a Spider** (Cronin, D., 2005, New York: Joanna Cotler Books).* This cleverly illustrated tale about the spider from **Diary of a Worm** continues in the same humorous style with something funny recorded for every day. After you have read it aloud, have the listeners talk about

FIGURE 29–1 The child asks the teacher to write in his journal: The caterpillar eating oranges, strawberries, apple, cucumber, and a cake.

what they would record for one of the days if they were a spider. Again, you can record what they say on a newsprint page. Then have them write/draw/scribble their own entry in their journal or literature log.

3. *Read the classic story* **The Very Hungry Caterpillar** (Carle, E., 1971, New York: Putnam). Children not only enjoy hearing about the caterpillar who eats an actual page hole through each of the fruits and a leaf before turning into a chrysalis and then a butterfly, but some want to make their own literary log of it. One child drew and labeled the name of each item the caterpillar ate. (See Figure 29–1.) If you can read his backward writing, you will note he added something extra: ice cream! The journal entry he asked the teacher to write for him read: "The caterpillar eating oranges, strawberries, apple, cucumber, and a cake."

SUGGESTED READINGS

Lindfors, J. W. (2008). *Children's language: Connecting reading, writing, and talk.* New York: Teachers College Press.

Soundy, C. S., Guha, S., and Qui, Y. (2007). Picture power: Placing artistry and literacy on the same page. *Young Children, 62*(3), 82–88.

Strickland, D. S., & Schickedanz, J. A. (2009). *Learning about print in preschool: Working with letters, words, and beginning links with phonemic awareness.* 2nd ed. Newark, DE: International Reading Association.

Messages

CONCEPT

Writing a simple message to someone else is an authentic writing experience many preschool children enjoy—especially because it is such a grown-up thing to do. Teachers who are aware of their children's writing skills often set up situations in which children have opportunities to write messages to other children telling them something that has happened, asking them a question, making a comment on something they did, or inviting them to do something or go somewhere. Whether or not the children can write is not the point. The message can be done in scribble writing or drawing.

One way to introduce children to message writing is to start with a daily message that you write for the whole class that asks for a response from the children as they arrive each day. It can be written on a large piece of unlined paper or newsprint clipped to a board or easel at the children's eye level. Paper is better than a write-and-wipe board since the message and responses can be preserved for review of the children's writing progress. Write the day and date at the top, and then your message. Save plenty of room for replies.

What if the youngsters do not know how to write a response? This may be the case with most of your children. Put out marking pens of different colors and encourage them to respond in scribble writing or drawing in any way they want. Even a dot is acceptable! Have them sign their names or initials after their response if they can. If they ask you for help, give them your support, but have them try to scribble, print, or draw their comments on their own.

Make the daily message a simple one based on a common experience that you read to the children, and invite those who want to write a response. For instance, you could write: *I rode to school this morning on my bike. It was fun*. Children can then scribble or draw their replies. Some may write a real word or two. Others may draw a bus or car or a person. Not everyone may be willing to try at first, but when they see what the others are doing and how enjoyable it is for them, they may eventually join in.

Be careful not to correct spelling or grammar in the children's responses. You want them to feel good about real writing and to continue with their efforts. As Shagoury (2009) reminds us, "Research in the

This child puts all her energy into writing a message.

field suggests a stance that is invitational, nurturing, and above all, respectful. It is crucial to respect young children's communication attempts, provide an environment rich in language, and be prepared to be awed by babies' and young children's capabilities" (p. 13).

As children become more adept at writing messages, have them think about writing a message to someone who is not present. You may need to work with individuals as they write messages to others, asking them to think about the other person who will receive it. When children are just beginning to write, they are often preoccupied with just getting anything down. They may not have thought about the other person at all. You may need to point out that their message is not for themselves but for another person.

Activities

1. Make message journals. Just as you made daily journals for the children to write in, change this to a "message journal" for individuals after the total group has had practice responding to your daily messages. Staple together and date five sheets of paper with the title "Message Journal" on the front. Then each morning one of the staff members can write a brief message at the top of a dated page for each child. Make it personal. For example: "Your new sneakers are cool" or "I like what you built in the block center." You can read your message for each child, and have them "write" or draw a response that they in turn read to you.

*2. Read **Nice Try, Tooth Fairy*** (Olson, M., 2000, New York: Simon & Schuster). This is a story full of messages—to the tooth fairy. Emma writes the first one as a thank-you letter for the money the tooth fairy left under her pillow after she lost her first tooth. But then she writes another message to get the tooth back to show her grandfather, who is coming for a visit. She gets a tooth but it is a hippo's tooth, so she has to write another message. She keeps getting the wrong teeth left under her pillow (skunk's, elephant's tusk, alligator's), and must write more letters, until finally her own little tooth turns up. But then she loses a second tooth! Have your children write their own messages to the tooth fairy.

*3. Read **A Letter to Amy*** (Keats, E. J., 1984, New York: HarperCollins) or ***Welcome to Kindergarten*** (Rockwell, A., 2001, New York: Walker). Sometimes a message is an invitation. In *A Letter to Amy*, Peter invites Amy to his birthday party. But he forgets to include all the important information. His mother points out that he didn't tell Amy when to come. So Peter writes "It is this Saturday at 2" on the back of the sealed envelope. In ***Welcome to Kindergarten***, the kindergarten teacher invites Tim to visit kindergarten, where he will be going next year. Have your children write an invitation.

*4. Read **Giggle, Giggle Quack*** (Cronin, D., 2002, New York: Simon & Schuster). In this hilarious Farmer Brown story the farmer goes on vacation and leaves his brother Bob in charge of the farm, but with a warning to watch out for the tricky Duck. He has written down instructions for Bob about all the animals. Duck overhears this conversation, finds a pencil, and writes his own instructions for Bob about serving pizza, bathing the pigs in bubble bath, and showing a TV movie for all of them. Then the phone rings and it's Farmer Brown who hears what is going on, and comes rushing home. After your children finish laughing have them write/scribble notes to Duck about what they think he should do.

SUGGESTED READINGS

Beaty, J. J., & Pratt, L. (2011). *Early literacy in preschool and kindergarten: A multicultural perspective.* 3rd ed. Boston: Pearson.

Bennett-Armistead, V. S., Duke, N. K., & Moses, A. M. (2005). *Literacy and the youngest learner: Best practices for educators of children from birth to 5.* New York: Scholastic.

Shagoury, R. E. (2009). *Raising writers: Understanding and nurturing young children's writing development.* Boston: Pearson.

31

Block Building

CONCEPT

Unit building blocks have long been one of the staple ingredients of early childhood programs. Children stack them up into towers; line them up as roads; build bridges, fire stations, hospitals, and zoos; and make corrals for their toy horses and garages for their cars. They first learn to *manipulate* blocks as 2- and 3-year-olds by filling up dump trucks or boxes and then dumping them out. They *master* their use by lining up rows of blocks over and over, and they finally learn to build *meaningful* structures through their playful self-discovery of the blocks. But what has this to do with literacy?

Literacy for preschool children involves speaking, listening, writing, and reading. Do children generally talk about their block-building activities? Although some builders may work in silence as they place one block on another, most children are eager, with a little encouragement, to relate what they plan to do, are doing, or have already done. Wellhousen and Giles (2005/2006) expand this concept to include skills fundamental to literacy: "Through their block play, children are introduced to crucial concepts needed for success in early literacy, including visual discrimination, use of abstract symbols, and oral language production. The block center also provides a context for reading and writing with a purpose" (p. 74).

Activities

Speaking

1. Take a photo. Take a photo of each completed block structure and ask the builders to tell you about it as you record on newsprint what they say.

2. Have reporters interview builders. Have children "reporters" interview each builder for the class newsletter by speaking into a tape recorder.

Unit blocks and block play help children learn about shapes of letters.

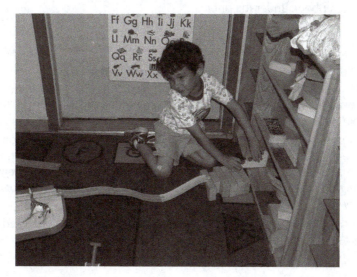

3. Ask the builders. Ask the builders what they are building that they saw on yesterday's field trip to a farm, zoo, fire station, or park, and so on. Can they tell you a story about it? Record it on newsprint.

Listening

1. Play back the tape. Play back the tape recording of the builder's interview for the group in the block center or for an individual listening with a headset.

2. Read a story. Read a story to children in the block center to motivate them to build something. Afterwards, leave the books in the block center for children to look at as they build. These or similar books are fine motivators:

> **Block City** (Stevenson, R. L., 2005, New York: Simon & Schuster)
>
> **Henry Builds a Cabin** (Johnson, D. B., 2002, Boston: Houghton Mifflin)
>
> **Iggy Peck, Architect** (Beaty, A., 2009, New York: Abrams)
>
> **This Is the Firefighter** (Godwin, L., 2009, New York: Hyperion)
>
> **This Is the House That Jack Built** (Taback, S., 2002, New York: G. P. Putnam's Sons)

Writing

To motivate children to write in the block center, put out writing materials such as paper of various sizes and colors for making signs and labels for the structures, adhesive notepads for messages about the buildings, and also pencils, markers, and tape. Include magazines with house plans, blueprints, and the books you have read. Your role is one of scaffolding, that is, providing a scaffold that supports children's capabilities beyond what they could achieve independently. You might suggest they use labels such as "under construction" or "work in progress." Or they may want to keep track of a lengthy building activity with a block center journal (Wellhousen & Giles, 2005/2006, p. 77).

1. Make signs for buildings. Put out pens and blank cards in the writing center for builders to make signs that identify each of their buildings in the block center. Print out the letters on a paper for children who want help in making their signs. Others may want to scribble their own signs. Mount the signs on the buildings. Take more photos.

2. Play the tape. Play the tape for the reporters who interviewed the builders for the class newsletter. Write down what each child said. Print or type out the "report" with headings. Post it on the children's bulletin board for children to look at.

3. Mount photos. Mount photos of the children's constructions in a scrapbook from the stories you have read. Have the builders dictate to you their own stories about the buildings as you write them down in the scrapbook under the photos.

Reading

1. Bring out the scrapbook. Bring out the scrapbook for the whole group to see. Ask the builders to read the stories they dictated under each photo. Most will remember the words they told you that you wrote, even though they are "reading" from memory and not from written words. Others may make up another story altogether. Accept whatever they say. It is a beginning for preliterate children.

2. Ask the reporters. Ask the reporters to "read" this week's newsletter from the bulletin board to one small group at a time. They also may be reading from memory. Each time they "read" their report to a different group, the reading process will become clearer for them. *Repetition* like this is a valuable ingredient in learning to read, just as it is in the mastery level of children's self-discovery play with new objects.

3. Ask who can read. Ask who can read the signs the builders have posted on their buildings. Have the builders tell them if they are correct (not incorrect).

4. *Read the same books.* Read the same books you read previously to another small group of children who would like to become the next builders in the block corner. Repeat the same activities with this group until all the children who want to have had a chance to be builders, reporters, story dictators, tape listeners, and readers.

SUGGESTED READINGS

Alexander, N. P. (2000). Blocks and basics. *Dimensions of Early Childhood, 28*(1), 29–30.

Chalufour, I., & Worth, K. (2004). *Building structures with young children.* St. Paul, MN: Redleaf Press.

Hewitt, K. (2001). Blocks as a tool for learning: Historical and contemporary perspectives. *Young Children, 56*(1), 6–13.

Wellhousen, K., & Giles, R. M. (2005/2006). Building literacy opportunity into children's block play: What every teacher should know. *Childhood Education, 82*(2), 74–78.

Wellhousen, K., & Kieff, J. (2001). *A constructivist approach to block play in early childhood.* Clifton Park, NY: Thomson/Delmar Learning.

32

Assessing Children's Writing

CONCEPT

As you look at the progress children have made in writing, one thing is sure to attract your attention: every child is different. Some children have trouble holding a writing implement. Others exhibit a strong grip but prefer to draw pictures instead of making letters. A few may create pages of scribble lines, one under the other, without a picture or letter in the lot. It is the same with reading. Some children show little interest in the words in a book but are fascinated by the pictures. It is up to you to plug into children's strong interests and help them progress from there.

When you note that certain children have little interest in reading but a strong desire to create writing that says something, support them in their quest. They may be the ones who come to reading through writing first. Have them scribble write what they want to say and read it back to you. Have them scribble write captions for pictures they have drawn and read them to you. Have them look at large-font words in picture books and experiment in writing their own words like that. Have them scribble write in their journal every day and read it to you. Have them scribble write responses to your daily messages and read them to you. Children learn to write by writing. When they eventually learn to write words anyone can read, they may suddenly want to read for themselves.

Drawing Can Lead to Writing

Other children may dislike writing but love to draw. Have them draw and draw and draw—all sorts of pictures. You can do the caption writing about their pictures at first if they agree. If they want to communicate something really important in their pictures you can help them decide the words to use. Write down a word or two and then ask them for help in what to say. Show them your words. Can they write any of these words?

Because drawing and writing both involve the use of an implement that makes marks, young children often do not differentiate between the two. Both drawing and writing are representational and thus

The teacher notes that the girl holds her pen in an immature "palmer grasp."

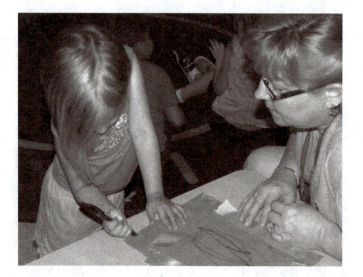

FIGURE 32–1 Caption Writing Progress.

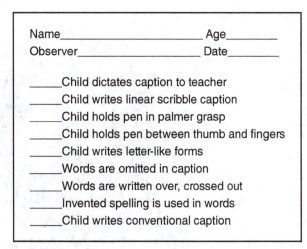

Name_____ Age_____
Observer_____ Date_____

_____Child dictates caption to teacher
_____Child writes linear scribble caption
_____Child holds pen in palmer grasp
_____Child holds pen between thumb and fingers
_____Child writes letter-like forms
_____Words are omitted in caption
_____Words are written over, crossed out
_____Invented spelling is used in words
_____Child writes conventional caption

need to be interpreted. Because young children have not learned how to represent all their ideas in words, they often draw pictures instead. You will need to look at children's drawings and captions to help you assess not only their sense of story, but how they are progressing in the writing process. (See Figure 32–1.)

Activities

1. Have everyone draw/write about a class project. Children in one class were learning about fruits and vegetables that make us strong. They visited a fruit orchard, a supermarket, and a roadside stand where fruits and vegetables were sold. The teacher read them the books ***Gathering the Sun*** (Ada, A.,1997, New York: Lothrop, Lee, & Shepard) in English and Spanish (see Strategy 27, "Dual Language Learners' Writing"), and ***Eating the Alphabet*** (Ehlert, L.,1989) with its large, delicious pictures of dozens of fruits and vegetables. The children talked about how fruits and vegetables made them strong—the boys emphasizing how they gave them muscles. Then the teacher asked them to draw a picture of their favorite fruits or vegetables and write a "story" about them.

Lilly drew separate pictures of each of her favorites and labeled them "strawberry," "pineapple," "kiwi," "corn," and "grape" and signed her name. (See Figure 32–2.) The teacher was delighted that she got them labeled properly. Could she also dictate a story? She told the teacher to write the following caption: "I told my mom to get these things from the store for me because they are good for me, and I like them."

FIGURE 32–2 I told my mom to get these things from the store for me because they are good for me, and I like them.

FIGURE 32–3 This is me with big muscles flying over my fruit boat.

The teacher liked the caption, but Mason complained that it wasn't a real story. It had to have a person in it. Then he proceded to draw a dramatic "something" with doors and "chimneys," colorful fruits around it, and a figure above it. (See Figure 32–3.) He dictated the following caption: "This is me with big muscles flying over my fruit boat." A boat, and a boy with big muscles! Yes, that was more like a story—a creative one.

When the children realized they could put themselves in their stories along with the fruits and vegetables they liked, many more caption pictures appeared. Emily drew herself and her sister, with the caption: "Me and my big sister taking a walk sharing an apple and an orange." (See Figure 32–4.)

Sharing these drawings and stories with the others in the class got everyone interested in making up pictures and stories of their own. Using caption pictures like this helps children to understand what writing is all about and to take the next step in the writing process. The teacher can then date and interpret these writings for her own progress report. Figure 32–1 is an observation checklist of children's picture-caption writing to help teachers assess how far along children have progressed in their writing.

Lilly with her spelled-out words is almost ready to write her own captions. The teacher decided to save her drawing and encourage her to continue the story, writing her own words.

Teachers using this checklist to interpret captions note that even scribbles indicate a step up in the progress from the child dictating and the teacher doing the writing. Crossed-out or written-over

FIGURE 32–4 Me and my big sister taking a walk sharing an apple and an orange.

words are also a sign of a child's progress in her writing, telling the teacher that the child is aware of the real words, and that she hasn't got it quite right but is trying. Such children are in the wonderful transition stage between writing in an "emergent" fashion and "conventional writing." What will it take for them to progress further? More pictures, more writing, and more practice. Be careful not to correct children in this stage as it may shut them down. Let them emerge on their own.

Mason may need more time with his writing, but his imagination has taken off. His little person figure with a circle for a head and two huge arm muscles may have been drawn to fit into the little space left after his large and dramatic fruit boat. Children who use invented spelling in their captions also indicate that they have developed *phonemic awareness*—perhaps without being taught. Their letters represent the word sounds (phonemes) they hear.

It is so important for teachers to give children authentic experiences, expecting and encouraging them to write and draw afterward. But don't let it end there. Read more picture books to them about the experience, and rather than sending their first drawings home, use these same drawings to generate more writing and more drawing.

*2. Read **Patches Lost and Found*** (Kroll, S., 2001, New York: Winslow Press). Here is a book written about a first grade girl, Jenny, but can easily be understood by younger children as well because of the large colorful illustrations and its message. Jenny loves to draw but doesn't like to write. When she has to write a story for homework, she asks if she can draw a picture instead, but the teacher says, "Not unless it goes with the words. Words first!"

Then Jenny's pet guinea pig, Patches, escapes, and she cannot find him either in the house or neighborhood. Her mother suggests she draw some posters showing Patches and her phone number and place them around the neighborhood. She writes "Patches Lost," along with her number, and papers her neighborhood with pictures. When he doesn't turn up for days, Jenny draws a series of imaginary pictures of a thief stealing him and getting caught by the police. When a man finally finds and returns Patches, Jenny's mother suggests that she write her story under her pictures and take them to school. She does, and her story is a great success, even teaching her teacher that it is okay to do pictures first and then words. For most preschool children, this is certainly the case.

Have your children try drawing pictures of a lost-and-found adventure of their own. Make it fun and funny. Can they write a few words? Even a lost-and-found pen as in ***The Little Red Pen*** (Stevens, J., 2011, Boston: Harcourt) can have an adventure! Then you can make a comprehensive assessment of their writing progress.

SUGGESTED READINGS

Baghban, M. (2007). Scribbles, labels, and stories: The role of drawing in the development of writing. *Young Children, 62*(1), 20–26.

Edwards, C. P., & Willis, L. M. (2000). Integrating visual and verbal literacies in the early childhood classroom. *Early Childhood Education Journal, 27*, 259–265.

Shagoury, R. E. (2009). *Raising writers: Understanding and nurturing young children's writing development.* Boston: Pearson.

Soundy, C. S., Guha, S., & Qiu, Y. (2007). Picture power: Placing artistry and literacy on the same page. *Young Children, 62*(3), 82–88.

Part III

Children's Reading

33 Emergent Reading

CONCEPT 1

Emergent reading, like emergent speaking and writing, is a natural process that occurs simultaneously with emergent writing. Some young children emerge into reading before they do any writing. Others begin with writing and then emerge naturally into reading. Are there any children who show few signs of emerging into either writing or reading? Yes. They are often the more active children who seldom sit still for anything and have paid little attention to any reading or writing activities going on around them—until now.

Now that they are in a preschool program, they and all the others can't help but become involved in the plethora of emergent literacy activities surrounding them: being read to, hearing book tapes and DVDs, chanting rhymes from books, singing songs from books, meeting characters from books, playing with character dolls and puppets, painting at an easel, scribbling captions under drawings, seeing environmental print, using the computer, labeling their block buildings, playing with sound words and alphabet letters, eating alphabet soup. And they love it—because it involves them personally, and it is fun! All you need to do is find out what the children's main interests are, and soon you will have them hooked.

Activities 1

Do they like trucks?

1. *Bring in your toy trucks and truck books.* What can children do with a truck in the classroom?

Roll it across the floor	Make up a song about it
Build a block road for it	Draw a picture of it
Make a block garage for it	Take digital photos of it
Make a ramp for it	Carry passengers in it

Children who make their own trucks like to make up their own stories about them.

See how far it will go	See how fast it will go
Play with it in the block center	Play with it in the sand table
Have a truck parade	Do the "truck shuffle" dance
Make up a story about it	Read a book about it, and more . . .

2. *Read books about trucks.* Did someone say, read a truck book?

    Dinotrux (Gall, C., 2009, New York: Little, Brown)

    Duck in the Truck (Alborough, J., 1999, New York: HarperCollins)

    I Love Trucks! (Sturges, P., 1999, New York: HarperCollins)

    My Truck Is Stuck! (Lewis, K., 2002, New York: Hyperion)

    Roadwork (Sutton, S., 2008, Somerville, MA: Candlewick)

    Tip Tip Dig Dig (Garcia, E., 2007, New York: Sterling)

    Truckery Rhymes (Scieszka, J., 2009, New York: Simon & Schuster)

    Trucks Roll! (Lyon, G. E., 2007, New York: Atheneum)

    Trucks Whizz! Zoom! Rumble! (Hubbell, P., 2003, New York: Marshall Cavendish)

    When Daddy's Truck Picks Me Up (Hunter, J. N., 2006, Morton Grove, IL: Whitman)

There are never too many truck books—and these are all for young children. You say that it's mainly boys who like trucks? Don't be too sure. What do you say about the verses in ***Truckery Rhymes***? Rita is a white ambulance; Gabby, a pink garbage truck; Rosie, a green wrecker; Lucy, a red ladder truck; and Izzy, an ice cream truck with a pistachio cone on top!

CONCEPT 2

Each of these books needs to be read again and again. From seeing the dazzling truck pictures and hearing their stories, you and the children can't help but create intriguing extension activities to keep each story going and emergent reading flowing: clapping out chants from the rhyming books, carrying animals to a zoo in the block center, driving toy trucks through a homemade tunnel, fastening a broom on a wagon for a street cleaner, scanning truck pictures and making homemade truck puzzles, making labels for the riding trucks, making stop and go signs for a truck parade, painting a cardboard carton as a truck to ride in with paper plate wheels, tape recording trucks sounds made by children and by real trucks, tabulating the number of trucks that pass by the window, inviting a truck driver to the class, painting truck pictures with captions, telling truck stories, scribbling in a truck diary, or going for a ride in a real truck.

Activities 2

Children come to love the words they hear in these books and want their favorites read over and over, so they can laugh at slurp-squelch, vroom-vroom, rumble-roar, putter-shriek, groan-creak. They want to play the roles of truck drivers, so have lots of hats available: mechanic hats, construction hats, firefighter hats, hardhats, police hats, tractor hats, baseball caps, cowboy hats. If you can't afford any, make your own: make hats out of folded newspaper, and have the children paint them to match their trucks.

1. *Have each child become a truck.* Scan pictures from the class's favorite books and laminate them for children to wear around their necks as they act out their roles. You can read their story aloud while they reenact the story.

2. *Do a shared writing activity.* Have each truck-child tell you what his or her truck does. Tape or take dictation and write down each story to be printed off and read back, first by you, and then by the child. Can he or she do it?

3. Find out each child's particular interest and bring in picture books on that topic. Make a list of possible book extension activities just as you did with truck books. Keep these activities going as long as the children's interest continues.

4. Keep track of the progression of each child's emergent reading activities. From listening to stories, participating in story activities, dictating their own stories, to reading their dictated stories, try to get every child involved. Reading their own stories is the important point here. As Vukelich and Christie (2009) discuss one of their children's stories, they say, "The fact that Eric was reading his own story made up of his own oral language ensured a successful reading experience. This emphasis on personal meaning is a hallmark of emergent literacy teaching strategies" (p. 10).

SUGGESTED READINGS

McVicker, C. J. (2007). Young readers respond: The importance of child participation in emerging literacy. *Young Children, 62*(3), 18–22.

Vukelich, C., & Christie, J. (2009). *Building a foundation for preschool literacy: Effective instruction for children's reading and writing development.* 2nd ed. Newark, DE: International Reading Association.

Book Center

CONCEPT

A comfortable, colorful place to find and look at a book is an essential ingredient in a preschool classroom. Children need to come together with books in as many creative ways as you can think of. Think outside the box! Think outside the traditional set of shelves. A book nook can be located in a corner with an awning canopy overhead, books hanging from colorful ribbons or strings held by a kitchen clip at one end. Posters or wall hangings featuring favorite book characters can decorate walls. A revolving shelf or "book spinner" from a store or library supply company such as Demco can entice more readers than do plain horizontal shelves. Ask parents to contribute an old but comfortable overstuffed chair to be used along with floor pillows and beanbag chairs.

Or make your book center into a "dinosaur den" with a fake palm or two from the Jurassic period, beanbag chairs as rocks, a large plastic pteranodon hanging from the ceiling, several toy dinosaurs lumbering along bookshelves containing a selection of books from Jane Yolen's *How Do Dinosaurs* series, such as *How Do Dinosaurs Say Good Night? How Do Dinosaurs Get Well Soon? How Do Dinosaurs Eat Their Food? How Do Dinosaurs Go to School?* You can make your own standup cutouts by scanning and enlarging dinosaur pictures. Dinosaur puppets from book stores or Demco may include velociraptor, tyrannosaurus rex, and pteranodon. Other book props such as character dolls, caps, capes, crowns, and magic wands should always be available to be taken out of the book center along with the books.

Children should be encouraged to read anywhere in the room. As Meier (2004) says, "It is most useful to have one central place from which children can choose books and other reading materials, and then other smaller areas to which children can take books and read alone or with a partner" (p. 67). Your whole classroom should be filled with book and reading ideas to bring children and books together. This is a new idea for many teachers who used to feel that books should be kept in the book center. With the new emphasis on emergent reading in preschool, the thinking now follows that of Baker and Schiffer (2007), who say: "Books can and should be sprinkled throughout the classroom interest areas so that they become an integral part of daily activities" (p. 44).

Keep books at children's eye level for their easy selection.

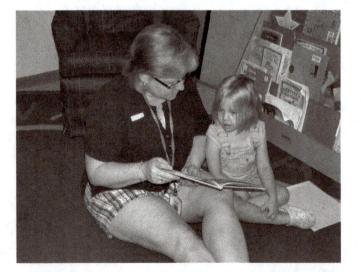

Activities

1. Have book posters made from book dust jackets mounted on the walls. Also make mobiles from the dust jackets and hang them from the ceiling. Have standup book character cutouts standing on the tops of room dividers. Change them as you bring in new books.

2. Make each of your learning centers into a book center. Use dust jacket posters of the books children can obtain from your central book center. Here are some of the books you might consider acquiring for each center:

Book Center

Miss Brooks Loves Books! (and I Don't) (Bottner, B., 2010)

Bats at the Library (Lies, B., 2008)

Born to Read (Sierra, J., 2008)

Wild about Books (Sierra, J., 2004)

Block Center

Henry Builds a Cabin (Johnson, D., 2002)

Iggy Peck, Architect (Beaty, A., 2009)

Thump, Quack, Moo (Cronin, D., 2008)

Block City (Stevenson, R., 2005)

Dramatic Play Center

Friday My Radio Flyer Flew (Pullen, 2008)

If I Had a Dragon (Ellery, T. & Ellery, A., 2006)

If Mom Had Three Arms (Orloff, K., 2006)

Violet the Pilot (Breen, S., 2008)

Manipulative Math Center

Max Counts His Chickens (Wells, R., 2007)

*We All Went on Safari** (Krebs, L., 2003)

A Second Is a Hiccup (Hutchins, H., 2004)

Mother Goose Numbers on the Loose (Dillon, L. & Dillon, D., 2007)

Music Center

I Love You! A Bushel and a Peck (Wells, R., 2005)

If You're Happy and You Know It (Warhola, J., 2007)

On Top of Spaghetti (Johnson, P., 2006)

She'll Be Coming 'round the Mountain (Emmett, J., 2006)

Art Center

Art (McDonnell, P., 2006)

Art and Max (Wiesner, D., 2010)

Pete the Cat (Litwin, E., 2008)

My Crayons Talk (Hubbard, P., 1996)

---

*Multicultural.

Science Center

Aaaarrgghh! Spider! (Monks, L., 2004)
*Big Bug Surprise** (Gran, 2007)
Carolina's Story (Rathmell, D., 2005)
I Love Bugs! (Dodd, E., 2010)

Large Motor Center

Hoops with Swoopes (Kuklin, S., 2001)
Luke Goes to Bat (Isadora, R., 2005)
Mike and the Bike (Ward, M., 2005)
Sally Jean, the Bicycle Queen (Best, C., 2006)

3. Make a card file of book extension ideas. As Bottini and Grossman (2005) tell us, "Centers provide children with opportunities for making choices, working with others, being involved in hands-on activities, and becoming fully engaged in learning" (p. 274). When children realize that fascinating books can be a part of each learning center in the classroom, they will become more eager than ever to get involved in reading activities.

SUGGESTED READINGS

Baker, I., & Schiffer, M. B. (2007). The reading chair: All interest areas need books, so spread those books around. *Young Children, 63*(3), 44–49.

Bottini, M., & Grossman, S. (2005). Center-based teaching and children's learning: The effects of learning centers on young children's growth and development. *Childhood Education, 81*(5), 274–277.

Meier, D. R. (2004). *The young child's memory for words: Developing first and second language and literacy.* New York: Teachers College Press.

Sipe, L. R. (2008). *Storytime: Young children's literary understanding in the classroom.* New York: Teachers College Press.

---

*Multicultural.

 Visual Literacy

CONCEPT 1

Visual literacy—what is it? You know how much young children enjoy looking at picture books. You understand that picture books are, in fact, the basic books for young children's emergence into reading. But as adults, we focus on the text of the books—the words and not the pictures. Learning to read means reading words, doesn't it? Not necessarily. For young children learning to read the pictures comes first. Remember, most children write in pictures before they write words. (See Strategy 22, "Caption Pictures.")

Most children read pictures, too, before they read words. For preschool children it is the pictures in the picture books that tell the story. They seldom pay any attention to the text until it is pointed out to them. This is visual literacy. As Johnson (2008) says, "Visual literacy is the ability to create visual messages and 'read' messages contained in visual communications" (p. 74).

Because we as adults read the text and not the pictures, text seems to us to be the most important feature of a book. Thus we have missed the point about the importance of children's understanding of pictures, their "visual literacy," in their development of reading skills. As Soundy and Qui (2006/2007) note: "Visual literacy is not even included in frameworks that identify the essentials of early literacy instruction!" (p. 70).

Visual literacy is not included because until recently few reading specialists have even looked for it. Kiefer, however, in her 1995 study of how children use picture books, notes that emergent readers in first and second grade tended to preview the illustrations in an entire picture book before beginning to read the text, and when they came to a word they didn't know, they glanced back at the illustrations for help (p. 21). By now reading specialists realize most preschool children believe it is the pictures in the book that tell the story. Children sometimes even inadvertently cover the text with an arm when being read to because they assume the teacher is reading from the pictures.

Is it then up to the teacher to set children straight about reading, to look at the words in the text, not the pictures? Are we to assume that visual literacy in children is not important and should be "corrected" as they emerge into reading? Not at all. Just the opposite is true. Visual literacy helps children extract meaning from words. It is an important step up the continuum of emerging into reading. Not only does it help readers to understand the meaning of the text, it also promotes their development of imagination, creative thought, and sense of story. We need to focus children's attention on illustrations and help them extract meaning from pictures as well as from words.

Visual literacy is especially important today because of the new forms of communication and new technology. Soundy and Qui (2006/2007) note: "To succeed in today's high-tech society, children will need to know how to make meaning not just from text but also from the vast amounts of information conveyed through images" (p. 83). Think of the icons on iPhones and iPads. Picture books do double duty in helping children extract this meaning. As Sipe (2008) tells us, "Words are best at describing relationships of details, pictures best at giving a sense of the whole" (p. 24).

But for helping young children learn to read, picture books perform the most important task of all: *helping children shift in their brains from their right hemisphere thinking to their left hemisphere*. Whereas pictures and visualization are a right-hemisphere function, words and reading are a left-hemisphere function. Young children initially operate from the right hemisphere. Thus, they must make a brain shift to the left hemisphere in order to learn to read words. Picture books serve this purpose. We must show the pictures to the children as we read the words. We must read these books aloud to children over and over, making sure they sit close enough to see the pictures—and see the words we are reading.

Afterwards we can leave the books in the reading center for the children to investigate on their own. Having a reading center full of wonderful picture books for children to look at is never enough. We must read these books aloud to children so they can see the pictures as they hear the words. We have long understood that reading is a left-brain function and that visualizing is a right-brain function. But we have missed the point about what can help children make this brain shift. Picture books are the key. Let us not neglect to read them daily to our young children.

Activities 1

1. Read picture books on a particular theme. A project on eating healthy foods can bring children together with pictures of all kinds of familiar and unfamiliar fruits and vegetables. As the project progresses read to small groups and individuals some of the following books, having children look carefully at the pictures. Can they pick out words that describe the pictures? Simple books are best.

> **Beach Day** (Lakin, P., 2004, New York: Dial)
>
> **I Will Never Not Ever Eat a Tomato** (Child, D., 2000, Cambridge, MA: Candlewick)
>
> **Fast Food** (Freymann, S., & Elffers, J., 2006)
>
> **Green Eggs and Ham** (Seuss, Dr., 1988, New York: Random House.)
>
> **Duck Soup** (Urbanovic, J., 2008, New York: HarperCollins)
>
> **Mud Tacos!** (Lopez, M., 2009, New York: Celebra)

2. Have children draw or create pictures to illustrate their favorite book. Preschool children do not copy book illustrations but create pictures from their own imaginations. Whatever they create is acceptable. Children in one classroom cut up pieces of orange, green, and brown foam and glued them onto backing paper to make vegetables for vegetable soup after hearing the book **Duck Soup**.

3. Read books about picky eaters. Have children talk about what foods they like and why they would eat them. Could they draw a picture about their favorite foods and why they would eat them? In one class, not to be outdone by the boys, Janette drew and dictated to the teacher: "I'm going in a space ship to pick a banana, an apple, a carrot, and strawberries to have big strong muscles." (See Figure 35–1.)

*4. Turn on children's imaginations by reading the Freyman book **Fast Food**.* It shows whimsical pictures of fruits and vegetables as zany forms of transportation (e.g., mushroom-on-a-peapod skateboard, red pepper fire engine, green zucchini train). Have the children draw their own pictures of fruit and vegetables doing unusual things. Brittany drew a carrot jumping rope. (See Figure 35–2.)

FIGURE 35–1 I'm going in a space ship to pick a banana, an apple, a carrot and strawberries to have big strong muscles.

FIGURE 35–2 A carrot is jumping rope.

FIGURE 35–3 I'm dancing and singing with my microphone and radio with a watermelon and apples.

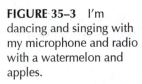

Denyce drew herself doing things with the fruit. (See Figure 35–3.) She dictated: "I'm dancing and singing with my microphone and radio with a watermelon and apples."

CONCEPT 2

After the children have drawn their pictures, have the children tell about them. How can they do it? Have them dictate a story to be printed off, or at least write a caption that they then can read over and over. Thus children themselves start with a picture and then create a text. Teachers find that focusing on book illustrations first is the way to help children emerge into reading text. Next comes helping children focus on the details of a book illustration to interpret what they mean. Visual literacy is more than just looking at pictures. It also involves interpreting what the pictures are telling us.

Activities 2

1. Have children in a small group go through the pictures in a book, page by page. Have them tell what they think the pictures are about. For example, look at the pictures in ***I Will Never Not Ever Eat a Tomato***. Then you can read the text illustrated by each picture. Do the children think the text and pictures fit together? Would they suggest any changes?

2. Have children look at the pictures they have drawn and the captions they have written. Do they think their text and pictures fit together? In one class, most of the children wanted to expand their captions. A few wanted to add new objects to their pictures. The children in Denyce's group wanted her to add more details to her caption about singing and dancing with a watermelon and apples. They wanted to know what song she was singing and what happened to the watermelon and apples. Did she eat them? One of the boys said: "Maybe they ate her." Everyone laughed, but that gave Denyce another idea. She sat down to draw about the apple that danced so hard it rolled down the street and about the watermelon that fell down, split open, and got squashed.

As their visual literacy improves children begin to see pictures and text from a new perspective. Pictures are not just "one thing." If you keep going with them, they can be a whole story. That's what a book is! These children were beginning to develop a real "sense of story."

SUGGESTED READINGS

Johnson, M. H. (2008). Developing verbal and visual literacy through experiences in the visual arts. *Young Children, (63)*1, 74–79.

Kiefer, B. Z. (1995). *The potential of picturebooks: From visual literacy to aesthetic understanding.* Upper Saddler River, NJ: Merrill/Prentice Hall.

Sipe, L. R. (2008). *Storytime: Young children's literacy understanding in the classroom.* New York: Teachers College Press.

Soundy, C. S., & Qui, Y. (2006/2007). Portraits of picture power: American and Chinese children explore literacy through the visual arts. *Childhood Education, 83*(2), 68–74.

Soundy, C. S., Guha, S., & Qui, Y. (2007). Picture power: Placing artistry and literacy on the same page. *Young Children, 62*(3), 82–88.

Children Reading Independently

CONCEPT

When young children first begin reading books on their own, most are not reading the words. They may be reading the pictures and making up the story as they go along. Or they may be telling the words of the story from memory as they turn the pages if it is a book that has been read to them repeatedly. You should be encouraged when you observe children involved in these behaviors, for it means they are on their way to becoming real readers.

If they enjoyed the experience, children who have been read to individually soon want to read on their own. When they first look at a picture book they may not even know how it works, turning the pages haphazardly and mumbling in a jargon that sounds like an adult reading. This is *pretend reading* or *book babble*. Not all young children do it, but some of those who have been read to frequently may start out by doing pretend reading. They may pretend to read books to their friends or even to dolls or stuffed animal toys.

Eventually they will be drawn to the pictures and assume it is the pictures that tell the story in the book. Now when they read a book they may point to the pictures and name them as they tell the story still in their own words. If you listen to their *picture-naming* stories you may note that they treat each page as a separate unit and not as a part of a continuing story. They have not yet developed what reading

Some children pretend to read books to their animal toys.

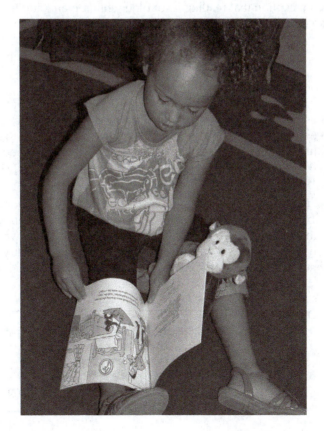

specialists call "a sense of story," that is, (1) that stories include a sequence of incidents describing the actions of the characters, and (2) that you must turn the pages of the book to learn what happens next.

On the other hand, certain young children who have been read to a great deal at home by sitting in the reader's lap and following the pictures in a favorite book closely as the story unfolds may be able to repeat all the words in that book almost verbatim. But a child who does this is not reading the words—she has memorized them. The fact that she can "read" a whole book in the words of the author is usually so exciting to her family that they make a big fuss about it, motivating her to really learn to read words.

Children learning to read storybooks demonstrate behaviors that appear to follow a developmental pattern, with their attention shifting from pictures to print and even their tone of voice changing. As Vukelich and Christie (2009) point out, "The intonation of children's voices when reading gradually shifts from sounding like they are telling an oral story to sounding like they are reading" (p. 7). A few children who have had a great deal of experience at home . . .

- by being read to,
- by having logos and signs pointed out to them,
- by being encouraged to draw and write stories and letters, and
- by using the computer on their own

may enter your classroom as true early readers. You may think they have been taught to read by someone at home, but most have not. They have "emerged" naturally into reading on their own.

Since you will not be teaching conventional reading to 3-, 4-, and 5-year-old children, what can you do to help as many children as possible "emerge into reading"? All 50 literacy strategies described in this book can assist you in this fascinating task, but helping children develop "a sense of story" may be as important as any of them. (See Figure 36–1.)

For children who still insist that they can't read a book, explain that they can read the story even if they are not sure of the words. They can read the pictures just as you do when the book is too long or complicated for the youngsters. As Teachout and Bright (2007) tell us, "Teachers must acknowledge and overcome the perception that reading is for older children and adults" (p. 106). To help children get started you can read to individuals or a small group a simple book by "reading the pictures" one page at a time.

Activities

1. *Read the pictures of* **Stuck in the Mud** (Clarke, J., 2007, New York: Walker). Simple books with big exciting pictures and repeated rhyming words are best. This book shows large pictures of a hen, a cat, a dog, a sheep, a horse, and a farmer on consecutive pages. All of them are trying to pull a little chick out of the mud, but get stuck themselves. The words "he pushed and he pulled again and again" are repeated. A surprise comes with a turnout page at the end that shows the little chick not being stuck at all.

Read the pictures to one small group of children at a time. Be sure everyone can see the pictures as you read. Then go back through the book and read the words. Now when you come to the repeated words, ask one of the children what they say. Run your finger under the words. Keep going through the book, asking another child to say the repeated words. Who wants to try it alone? Give the book to that child and have her read. Accept whatever she says. Let each child have a turn, having the

FIGURE 36–1 Developing
a Sense of Story.

- Choose books with easily followed plots, pictures.
- Read books to individuals over and over.
- Ask listeners what comes next.
- Help listeners to "read the pictures."
- Give children time to look at book on their own.

others help if that child gets stuck. Whether they recognize the words or not, repeated readings help them memorize them—one of the first steps toward independent reading.

2. Read the same story again and again. Children develop a sense of story by hearing stories read to them over and over. The books themselves need to be exciting stories with easily followed plots in explicit sequences that the children can understand. They need to sit close to the reader so they can see the pictures and follow along.

3. Have children participate in story reading. Choose books with words and plots that will interest the children. Stop in the middle of an exciting part and ask the children, "What do you think will happen next?" Talk about the story afterward by going over the plot sequence in fun ways. Then you need to give children the opportunity and time to look at the book on their own, and perhaps try to read it to a friend.

4. Read **Pete the Cat, I Love My White Shoes** (Litwin, E., 2010, New York: Harper). This is a simple story with a large black cat walking along singing his song about loving his white shoes, then his red shoes (from stepping in strawberries), then his blue shoes (from stepping in blueberries), then his brown shoes (from stepping in mud), but does Pete cry after each incident?

"Goodness, no!" How do your listeners think it will end? A number of children will quickly be able to read this story independently if you challenge them. Have someone reenact the story as it is being read.

5. Read **Chick 'n' Pug** (Sattler, J., 2010, New York: Bloomsbury). Here is another simple story about a little chick who is bored in the chicken coop, so off he goes looking for adventures like his hero in the book "The Adventures of Wonder Pug." He finds a pug who is hardly a wonder dog, but who only wants to sleep. One line of text on the bottom of each page keeps the story going. How does Chick save the day? Stop and ask your listeners. After the second reading challenge a child to read the book.

SUGGESTED READINGS

Meier, D. R. (2000). *Scribble, scrabble: Learning to read and write.* New York: Teachers College Press.

Morrow, L. M., Freitag, E., & Gambrell, L. B. (2009). *Using children's literature in preschool to develop comprehension: Understanding and enjoying books.* 2nd ed. Newark, DE: International Reading Association.

Teachout, C., & Bright, A. (2007). Reading the pictures: A missing piece of the literacy puzzle. *Young Children, 62*(4), 106–107.

Vukelich, C., & Christie, J. (2009). *Building a foundation for preschool literacy: Effective instruction for children's reading and writing development.* 2nd ed. Newark, DE: International Reading Association.

37 Computer Books

CONCEPT

Does the computer have a place in an early childhood literacy program? It does. Simple computer programs based on a concept you are featuring in other learning centers can support and extend children's learning. If the computer program is based on a children's book, the ideas gained from the computer will be reinforced every time children look at the book.

While some teachers may view the computer with reluctance because it is such a high-tech piece of equipment, most young children are excited to try it out with their natural "hands-on" learning style. If you observe them, you will see them figuring it out by trial and error. At first everyone will want a turn. Each day, you can demonstrate to a small group the basics of how to use the computer and then let them try it on their own.

After the novelty wears off, two children at a time can choose to use the computer during the free choice period by wearing the two computer necklaces you provide. Others can "sign up" for a turn on a numbered sheet. Give computer users enough time to get deeply involved. Setting a timer for five minutes each is not enough time for real learning to take place. Onlookers can also benefit. Anderson (2000) found that children, even onlookers, spoke more when observing computer users than they did when observing other activities.

Set up your computer center away from classroom traffic. It can be located in its own center, in the writing center, in the science/discovery center, or in any other area where software programs support similar learning activities. Have the monitor and printer on a low table near a wall outlet so cords are kept out of children's reach. Be sure the monitor is at a child's eye level while seated and not above it. Place two child-size chairs in front of the monitor to encourage two children to interact. These pairs can learn

- To take turns with the mouse
- To converse with one another about what they see and hear
- To teach each other how a program works
- To problem-solve together

Two children at a time can choose to use the computer during free choice period.

FIGURE 37–1 Choosing
Computer Softwares.

> - Tried out by teacher ahead of time
> - Based on children's books being used
> - Attractive to young children
> - Easily used and understood by children
> - Teaches appropriate skills
> - Lead-in to learning center activities

Software Programs

Choose the software programs carefully. It is important for your literacy program that the software you choose can be integrated into the classroom learning centers. (See Figure 37–1.) As with book tapes, CDs, and videos, computer programs are more abstract than the concrete materials that are more appropriate for children's learning. But computer programs can be lead-ins to hands-on, concrete activities in the learning centers.

Each computer CD-ROM can be based on a children's book you have available in the book center. It is also important that you try out the software to make sure it is at an appropriate level, contains activities attractive to the children, teaches skills you want children to learn, and can lead to hands-on activities in the learning centers.

Dual Language Computer Storybook Programs

For children who are learning English as a second language along with their own home language, computer storybook CD-ROMs can be extremely helpful. Most of these programs show the pages of the real books with read-alongs in both languages. With a click of the mouse, the listeners can switch from one language to another. It is important to have the real book available along with its computer program so that the children can look at the book after using the computer program. The following CD-ROMs are available from www.childrenssoftwareonline.com:

> *Just Grandma and Me* CD-ROM (English, French, German, Spanish)
>
> *Harry and the Haunted House* CD-ROM (English, Spanish)
>
> *Little Monster at School* CD-ROM (English, Spanish)
>
> *Ruff's Bone* CD-ROM (English, Spanish)
>
> *The Tortoise and the Hare* software (English, Spanish)

Activities

1. Help children become familiar with the computer.

- How to turn it on
- How to wait until the main menu appears
- How to double click the mouse on the proper menu icon
- How to wait until the program menu appears
- How to click on the activity they wish to pursue

You will already have installed the program they are to use either by installing it on the hard drive or by showing the children how to run the program by inserting its disk into the disk drive, waiting for the program menu, and clicking on a game or activity.

*2. Read **Miss Spider's Tea Party** (Kirk, D., 1994, New York: Scholastic).* Here is one model you can follow for many of the book/computer programs. It is important to read this book to individuals or small groups of children a number of times so they will become familiar with it before using the computer program. Large, colorful cartoon-like illustrations on every other page show Miss Spider, a yellow garden spider, inviting various insects to her party. Two timid beetles, three fireflies, four bumblebees, six ants, seven butterflies, and nine spotted moths all refuse her rhyming invitations and flee as fast as possible. They do not want to end up as food for the spider. Finally, a little moth learns that Miss Spider wants only to be friends. He tells the other insects and they all return for the party.

3. Discuss the story with the children. Your listeners should enjoy the clever pictures of the insects and be excited to talk about the story. Does Miss Spider look scary? What about the other insects? Why are they afraid of Miss Spider? What makes them change their mind? What does Miss Spider really eat at her party? There are many new words and phrases the children will want to hear again: gloomy nook, jolly mugs, mortal dread, floral centerpiece—words that sound great. The pictures will help the children learn to decipher their meanings. Now they are ready for the computer program.

*4. Play **Miss Spider's Tea Party** CD-ROM (Scholastic).* Help the computer partners to sign in their names at the beginning of the program and then choose the level of difficulty of the games: easy, medium, or hard. Novice users should start with easy. Miss Spider asks the player to invite an insect to the party from the images at the bottom of the screen: ant, butterfly, bee, beetle, cricket, firefly, caterpillar and moth, or grampy spider. Players can print a guest list from the main menu to help them keep track of their progress, and when all the guests are assembled, they can print their own invitation with your help.

5. Participate in activities based on the story. Afterwards children can carry these activities into other learning centers by counting plastic insects, starting an ant farm in the math/science center, painting insects or making Play-Doh models in the art center, reenacting the story in the book center, having a tea party in the dramatic play center, dictating a story in the writing center, or going outside to look for butterflies and their cocoons or chrysalises.

*6. Read **Stellaluna** (Cannon, J., 1993, San Diego: Harcourt).* Although the story is longer than those in many of the picture books described in this text, children enjoy hearing it read and following the adventures of the "upside down" baby bat who falls into a bird's nest by accident and learns to live like a bird in the African jungle. The computer program focuses on the reading of the story, illustrated by wonderfully animated sound graphics. Children can choose to hear the story read, to click on objects in the scenery while the story is read, or to play a bat quiz.

7. Click on objects in the jungle scene. Words in the text are highlighted and vocalize or move when clicked on. Children often invent their own game of clicking on objects in the jungle scene (elephants, giraffe, monkey, hippo, caterpillar, moth, bats, trees) to see how many they can make move. Their partner may discover that clicking on the same object more than once results in several surprising moves. Children learn new words, word recognition, and facts about bats. They also consider the idea that animals that look very different can have the same feelings.

8. Play with African animals in block area, or with bat doll for story reenactment. Put out plastic African animals in the block area to see what kind of play ensues. A cloth bat doll can be ordered from Demco, or children can make their own bat wings to be used in story reenactments.

Research has determined that interactive storybook software like the sampling in Figure 37–2 is important because it offers children active participation in their own learning, consistent with the theories of Piaget and Vygotsky (Glasgow, 1996).

FIGURE 37–2 CD-ROM
Living Books.

Arthur's Teacher Trouble	*Harry and the Haunted House*
Arthur's Birthday	*Just Grandma and Me*
Arthur's Computer Adventure	*Little Monster at School*
Arthur's Reading Race	*Ruff's Bone*
Dr. Seuss ABCs	*Stellaluna*
Dr. Seuss Cat in the Hat	*Tortoise and the Hare*
Dr. Seuss Green Eggs and Ham	

SUGGESTED READINGS

Anderson, G. T. (2000). Computers in a developmentally appropriate curriculum. *Young Children, 55*(2), 90–93.

Beaty, J. J., & Pratt, L. (2011). *Early literacy in preschool and kindergarten: A multicultural perspective.* 3rd ed. Boston: Pearson.

Glasgow, J. N. (1996). It's my turn! Motivating young readers. *Learning and Leading with Technology, 24*(3), 20–23.

Robinson, L. (2003). Technology as a scaffold for emergent literacy: Interactive storybooks for toddlers. *Young Children, 58*(6), 42–48.

Smith, C. R. (2001). Click and turn the page: An exploration of multiple storybook literacy. *Reading Research Quarterly, 36*(2), 152–183.

38 Shared Reading

CONCEPT

Shared reading, a strategy more often used in older children's reading programs, can just as easily be applied to book reading with children in early childhood programs. The concept of shared reading originated in the home where an adult reads to a child in an intimate setting, and the child feels free to interrupt or ask questions without ruining the story for others. Shared reading in the classroom attempts to recreate this intimate atmosphere of the home. Morrow, Freitag, and Gambrell (2009) point out that sharing books enhances children's background knowledge, develops their sense of story structure, and familiarizes them with the language of books: "The language of books differs from oral language and provides a model for speaking" (p. 45). In other words, shared reading emphasizes teachers modeling how to read.

Then children join in the reading, interacting with the teacher and helping the teacher read. Children's responses to the oral reading are the most important aspect. Shared reading is similar to read-alouds, but it purposely encourages children to express their reactions to the story. Sometimes the teacher thinks his or her role comes first. But as McVicker (2007) tells us, "It is important to encourage and pay attention to children's spontaneous responses such as asking questions, joining in with repeated phrases, filling in the blanks, and moving like one of the characters" (p. 19). Your goal in shared reading is to engage the children in the story like this.

First and foremost, you must select appropriate books. Many teachers use "big books," the oversized editions of familiar books—large enough for children to see the print as well as the pictures. (See Strategy 40, "Big Books.") When these books are used with small groups, the children can follow along as the reader draws her finger under the words. She can stop at any time and engage the children in a dialogue about the characters or plot. If the story is predictable the reader can ask the

These children help the teacher read the story.

122

FIGURE 38–1   Big Books
from Lakeshore
(1-800-778-4456).

> *Brown Bear, Brown Bear, What Do You See?*
> *Caps for Sale*
> *Five Little Monkeys Jumping on the Bed*
> *Flower Garden*
> *If You Give a Mouse a Cookie*
> *Is Your Mama a Llama?*
> *Silly Sally*
> *Saturday Night at the Dinosaur Stomp*

children to guess what is coming next. Figure 38–1 provides a sampling of big books available from Lakeshore.

Predictable books contain stories that rhyme, are full of repetition, or have sequential patterns that children can follow. (See Strategy 41, "Predictable Books.") Shared reading like this takes some children to the next step in emerging into reading. With repeated readings from predictable books they may begin to learn the lines of several stories by heart.

When children realize it is not the pictures but the print that tells the story, some of them may want to figure out how the print tells the reader what to say. They may point to one of the words and ask the reader what it says. The reader in turn may point to other words the children know by heart and ask them what they say. No matter what happens in shared reading sessions, they need to be informal and fun. As Neuman and Roskos (1993) note, "In these settings, there is a spirit of collaboration as teachers and children work together in constructing meaning in stories" (p. 91).

Activities

Some teachers prefer to place the big book on an easel facing the children while reading it. Be sure to have at least one copy of the regular-size book available for children to look at and compare with the big book. Here is a more detailed activity for **Five Little Monkeys Jumping on the Bed**.

1. Read the big book **Five Little Monkeys Jumping on the Bed** (Christelow, E., 1989, Boston: Houghton Mifflin). Show children in a small group of six the cover of the book at first and ask them what they see. Read the story all the way through without a pause. Next time through, ask the children to repeat in unison what the doctor says the five different times: "No more monkeys jumping on the bed!" Count off the children 1 through 5 to represent the monkeys. Ask the sixth child to be the mother.

Next time through, have the five children stand up and jump up and down as described in the book. When one falls down, have that child sit down. At the same time, have all the children repeat the doctor's words. By now, most of the children will know the story by heart. Have them remain seated this time and say as much of the story in unison as they can. Finally, close the book and see if they can say the story in unison without the book while jumping.

2. Look for word recognition from **Five Little Monkeys**. Another day, print out six signs on cards saying "MONKEY #1," "MONKEY #2," "MONKEY #3," "MONKEY #4," "MONKEY #5," and "MOTHER." With the children seated, ask if anyone can find the word "monkey" in the book as you read it together. Give that child the MONKEY #1 card to hold. Continue reading and ask the same question each time you come to the same word. Can they tell the difference between the word "monkey" and "mother"? Read this book to other groups of six children until everyone has had the chance to learn the story and pick out the words.

SUGGESTED READINGS

Beaty, J. J., & Pratt, L. (2011). *Early literacy in preschool and kindergarten: A multicultural perspective.* 3rd ed. Boston: Pearson.

McVicker, C. J. (2007). Young readers respond: The importance of child participation in emerging literacy. *Young Child, 62*(3), 18–22.

Morrow, L. M., Freitag, E., & Gambrell, L. B. (2009). *Using children's literature in preschool to develop comprehension: Understanding and enjoying books.* Newark, DE: International Reading Association.

Neuman, S. B., & Roskos, K. A. (1993). *Language and literacy learning in the early years: An integrated approach.* Fort Worth, TX: Harcourt.

39 Dual Language Readers

CONCEPT

Dual language readers, like dual language writers, can emerge into reading by discovering how it works. (See Strategy 27, "Dual Language Learners' Writing.") They can also learn to write in both their home language and English through discovery. As Shagoury (2009) tells us, "Young dual language learners actively figure out the way the written language works in their first and second language" (p. 53). Once children learn literacy in their home language they do not need to relearn these skills in school.

However, most of the youngest learners have not yet learned to read in any language. It is up to you and your staff to give them tools to help. Give them many opportunities to improve their writing skills, which simultaneously develop with reading skills. Reading their own writing is one of the keys to reading texts. Your reading of bilingual books is another key.

Do not downplay their home language. Figure 27–1 gives suggestions on helping dual language children learn to write. These ideas also help them learn to read. Start with simple bilingual books at first. Pair the dual language learner with an English-speaking youngster to begin their own reading. Put out several simple bilingual books for them to choose from. Also include books with a copy in English and one in Spanish. (See Figure 39–1.)

At first the books on your shelf for dual language learners should be simple, fun picture books that children will want to look at and have no trouble following. Select a minimum of books to give the children a chance to see each book separately with its cover facing out on a low bookshelf. Putting out too many books is confusing for children and requires a longer time for each pair to select the book they want. Learning for young children takes time, you remember, and repetition is important. Do not be surprised if one pair selects the same book day after day. They are at the *mastery* level of self-discovery and need to try out their new learnings again and again.

You can "picture-walk" through a book before reading the words.

FIGURE 39–1 Books to
Help Bilingual Readers.

> *Bebé Goes Shopping* (Elya, S., 2006)
>
> *I Love Saturdays y domingos* (Ada, A., 2002)
>
> *Is Your Mama a Llama?* (Guarino, D., 1989)*
>
> *Margaret and Margarita* (Reiser, L., 1993)
>
> *Tortillas and Lullabies* (Reiser, L., 2008)
>
> *The Very Hungry Caterpillar* (Carle, E., 1971)*
>
> _____
>
> *separate books in each language

Activities

1. Have each pair choose one of the books. Have them each go through the book slowly, one page at a time, looking at the pictures left to right. Can either of them tell what their book is about? Would anyone like to "picture-read" his book to his partner? Encourage both partners to picture-read to each other in either language. You can observe and listen.

2. Read book to whole class. Read each of these books to the whole class, one at a time, day after day. Start by doing a "picture walk" where you go through the illustrations, pointing to them and telling what they are (Gillanders & Castro, 2011, p. 93). Then read the sentences.

*3. Read **Tortillas and Lullabies** (Reiser, L., 1998, New York: Greenwillow Books).* Every four pages show a little girl's great-grandmother doing something for her grandmother, the grandmother doing something for her mother, the mother doing something for the little girl, and the little girl doing something for her doll. Every time this activity is the same, but different. Full-page folk art shows these family members making tortillas, gathering flowers, washing a dress, and singing a lullaby. A sentence at the top of the page is in English. A similar sentence at the bottom is in Spanish.

First have your pair of listeners try reading aloud the pictures. Then you should read the simple sentence on each page with your pair of listeners following the words as you move your finger along, first saying words in English, then the same thing in Spanish. Have them repeat each sentence after you have read it aloud. If they stumble, do it again. Finally, have them read the book to each other as best they can. Then do another book. Other simple bilingual books can be used to help your children learn to read in the same manner.

SUGGESTED READINGS

Gillanders, C., & Castro, D. C. (2011). Storybook reading for young dual language learners. *Young Children, 66*(1), 91–95.

Nemeth, K. N. (2009). *Many languages, one classroom: Teaching dual and English language learners.* Beltsville, MD: Gryphon House.

Shagoury, R. (2009). Language to language: Nurturing writing development in multilingual classrooms. *Young Children, 64*(2), 52–57.

Shin, S. J. (2010). Teaching English language learners: Recommendations for early childhood educators. *Dimensions of Early Childhood, 38*(2), 13–20.

Big Books

40

CONCEPT

Big books are oversized paperback picture books originally made by primary teachers for the purpose of teaching conventional reading. They are used mainly in reading groups for shared reading. In elementary schools, groups often hold regular-size copies of the big book, which they follow as the teacher or other students read from the big book. The large size of the books (14 ½ by 18 inches) makes it possible for all the students in the group to see the pictures and large print of the story as it is read aloud and for the teacher to point out particular words and sentences. The original teacher-made big books were often traditional tales with predictable patterns of language such as *The Three Little Pigs*.

Today, commercial book publishers have reproduced numerous children's trade paperback books (the books discussed in this text) as big books, since reading programs depend more and more on children's literature rather than on traditional basal readers to teach reading. Big books with predictable stories have caught on in both elementary reading programs and more recently in preschool classrooms. Morrow, Freitag, and Gambrell (2009) talk about big books being effective for developing children's concepts about books because of their size: "As the teacher reads the book and tracks the print from left to right across the page, children see that books are for reading. They notice where to begin to read on a page and learn to differentiate the print from the pictures. Children begin to realize that the reader's spoken words are being read from the print in the book" (p. 41).

Preschool children love to hold these giant-size books and leaf through them to look at the pictures. Teachers of young children, however, need to be aware that they will not be using big books as elementary teachers do. It is not developmentally appropriate to teach conventional reading in preschool, but instead to involve children in emergent literacy. Some teachers do read to small groups of preschool children from big books in a shared reading experience. (See Strategy 38, "Shared Reading.") Often, however, preschool teachers get down on the floor with the children and interact with them without a large book blocking their vision.

Put the big book on a stand to read it with your hands free for gestures.

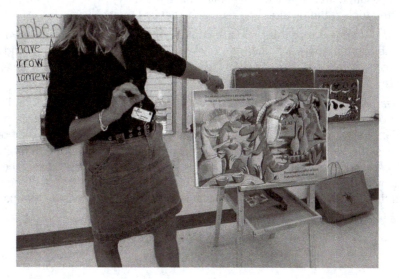

FIGURE 40–1 Big Books
from Scholastic.

> *Caps for Sale*
> *Five Little Monkeys Jumping on the Bed*
> *Is Your Mama a Llama?*
> *The Itsy Bitsy Spider*
> *Mama, Do You Love Me?*
> *Miss Mary Mack*
> *Mrs. McNosh Hangs up Her Wash*
> *Saturday Night at the Dinosaur Stomp*
> *Silly Sally*
> *There Was an Old Lady Who Swallowed a Fly*
> *The Three Billy-Goats Gruff*

Preschool programs with limited budgets need to consider carefully how many big books they will purchase, since they are more expensive than regular-size books. It is more important for preschools to have a well-stocked library of regular children's literature picture books than a great many big books. You will want a few for the children to handle on their own, especially when you have read the same story from a regular-size book. Also, children with vision impairments may be able to see the large print in the big books. Keep some big books on hand for the times you will be reading to a total group, for shared reading activities, and for children to be able to handle on their own in the book center. Figure 40–1 offers a list of big books published by Scholastic.

Activities

Be sure the big books you purchase are simple stories with fast action, rhyming, and repetition. Then you can get the children involved in playing word games with them. Put the big book on a stand or an easel so you have your hands free and the small group you work with can see the page and pictures clearly.

1. Read **Silly Sally** (Wood, A., 1992, San Diego: Harcourt). Set the book on a stand or easel and gather the children around you. The children should already be familiar with the book, having heard you read the regular-size book many times. You can stand next to the book and read the first page: "Silly Sally went to town, walking backwards, upside down." Ask if any child in the group can walk *backwards* and let them demonstrate. Now each child can try. Continue turning the pages and reading until you come to the next action (i.e., dancing a jig). Ignore the "upside down" part, but ask who can *dance* a jig like the pig and have them try. Go through the entire book like this, having children look at the pictures and repeat the actions themselves.

The next time you read this big book, run your hand under the words as you read them, and ask if anyone can find the words that say "backwards," "dancing," "leaping," and so on. They have heard the words; they have demonstrated the words; now some of them may be able to find the printed words. Can anyone do it? Let them try.

2. Read **Mrs. McNosh Hangs Up Her Wash** (Weeks, S., 1998, New York: Harper). Read the regular-size book to the children, who will love the rhythm and rhyming on each page. For the big-book version, bring in a clothes basket with several items in it as shown in the book (e.g., a dress, newspaper, stuffed animal dog, bat from *Stellaluna*, wreath, letter, apron). String a clothes line with clothespins across the back of the reading center at the children's level. Then as you read the story page by page, have one of the children pick an appropriate item out of the basket and hang it up. Next time through the story, see who can find the word on the page that names the item they have hung up.

SUGGESTED READINGS

Beaty, J. J., & Pratt, L. (2011). *Early literacy in preschool and kindergarten: A multicultural perspective.* 3rd ed. Boston: Pearson.

Cowley, J. (1991). The joy of big books. *Instructor, 101*(3), 19.

Morrow, L. M., Freitag, E., & Gambrell, L. B. (2009). *Using children's literature in preschool to develop comprehension: Understanding and enjoying books.* Newark, DE: International Reading Association.

Warner, L. (1990). Big books and how to make and use them. *Day Care and Early Education. 18*(1), 16–19.

Predictable Books

41

CONCEPT

Predictable books are picture books with repetitive words or phrases (see Figure 41–1), rhyming words and rhythmic cadences (see Figure 41–2), cumulative episodes (see Figure 41–3), or sequential patterns (see Figure 41–4). Children are captivated by their catchy rhythms and rhymes. They are able to chime in and follow along as an adult reads the story, and then to guess (predict) what comes next when the reader pauses. Predictable books are thus most effective in promoting young children's development of "sense of story," as well as independent reading and retelling of stories. Hearing the stories over and over, children seem to memorize the rhyming words without even trying.

The texts of some predictable books are like advertising jingles: so catchy you can't get them out of your head. The youngest children may still think you are reading the pictures as the story progresses, but little by little they come to realize it is the words themselves and not the pictures that tell the story. Fill your classroom with predictable books. You can't have too many. A guide for selecting predictable books from this text can be found in Figure 41–5.

As you look at the titles of these books, you will soon discover still another reason children love predictable books. They are so much fun! Whenever you see the title of a book that rhymes or sounds nonsensical, it may very well be a predictable book. Figure 41–5 lists criteria found in many, but not

This girl chooses a predictable book every time.

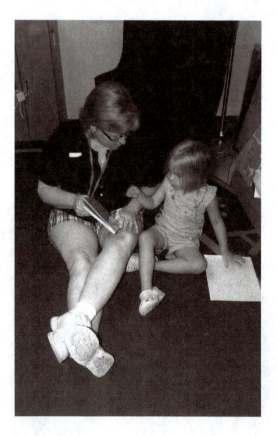

FIGURE 41–1 Repetitive Words and Catchphrases.

Alligator Baby (Munsch, R., 1997)

I'm Your Bus (Singer, M., 2009)

Snip Snap, What's That? (Bergman, M., 2005)

Is Your Mama a Llama? (Guarino, D., 1989)

Miss Mary Mack (Hoberman, M., 1998)

FIGURE 41–2 Rhyming Words; Rhythmic Cadences.

Giraffes Can't Dance (Andreae, G., 1999)

Llama Llama Misses Mama (Dewdney, A., 2009)

Grumpy Gloria (Dewdney, A., 2006)

Bats at the Library (Lies, B., 2008)

Twist with a Burger, Jitter with a Bug (Lowery, L., 1995)

FIGURE 41–3 Cumulative Episodes.

Drat That Fat Cat! (Thomson, P., 2003)

Stuck in the Mud (Clarke, J., 2007)

Roar of a Snore (Arnold, M., 2006)

Down by the Cool of the Pool (Mitton, T., 2001)

all, predictable books. Morrow, Freitag, and Gambrell (2009) tell us predictable books are ideal for shared reading because they invite children to respond: "They allow the child's first experience with reading to be enjoyable and successful with minimal effort." Because repeated readings promote children's independent reading, "children can confidently revisit a familiar book without adult assistance" (pp. 46–47).

You may already have in mind which predictable books you want to read to your children because they are the very books both you and the children already enjoy hearing over and over. Review your books and decide which ones to start with. Do some already appeal to the children because of the rhythm and rhyming? These are the ones most easily memorized unintentionally by certain children as they hear them read again and again. If they have large-font print as well, some of the children may recognize and remember these words when you reread the story. For many children, predictable books are the key in learning to read.

Activities

1. Read one of the books from the first group (repetitive words and catchphrases). **Alligator Baby** (Munsch, R., 1997, New York: Scholastic) is the fanciful story of Kristen's mother who has her baby, by mistake, in a zoo. She comes home with a baby that Kristen soon sees by its tail, claws, and face, is not a people baby. It's an alligator baby! So her mother returns to the zoo to claim her human baby, but always seems to come back with the wrong one—until Kristen saves the day. Your children will want to reenact this story either by taking the roles of the various animal babies (alligator, seal, gorilla), or by being the mother, with stuffed animals for the babies. Then three other children will need to appear as the real zoo animals who come barging in to claim their babies. Children love to reenact this story with all of its sounds: *aaahaaaa* when a nose gets bit, and *blam, blam, blam, blam* when the door gets knocked. You will need to talk with the children about what could really happen in such a story. Is it all make-believe? How did Kristen finally find her baby brother? What might happen next?

FIGURE 41–4 Sequential Patterns.

> *Five Little Monkeys Jumping on the Bed* (Christelow, E., 1989)
> *The Lady with the Alligator Purse* (Westcott, N., 1988)
> *My Truck Is Stuck* (Lewis, K., 2002)

FIGURE 41–5 Choosing Predictable Picture Books.

- Words should be repetitive, rhyming, or rhythmic.
- Text may have cumulative episodes.
- Text may use number or letter sequences.
- Text should be brief and fast-paced.
- Pictures should illustrate words.
- Story should feature engaging humans or animals.

2. Read one of the books from the second group (rhythmic cadences). **Twist with a Burger, Jitter with a Bug** (Lowery, L., 1995, Boston: Houghton Mifflin) has catchy words, snappy rhythm, and collage-like characters in a riot of color that captivate most listeners. Simple text in large-font words (*dance a mambo* on the first page and *snap to a rap* on the second) alert children to the rhyme to follow (*put on your cleats and tap, tap*). Read this to a small group a second time and have them dance or clap to the rhythm. Can they wait till you get to the funniest rhyme of all about boogying in the bathtub, the hula-hula dance, and rumba if you wanna in your underpants? This book may become one of their favorites, and some children will memorize it after hearing it over and over.

3. Read one of the books from the third group (cumulative episodes). **Down by the Cool of the Pool** (Mitton, T., 2001, New York: Orchard) has a population of wildly gyrating critters: a frog (wheee!), a duck (flap), a pig (wiggle), a sheep (stamp), a cat (bound), a dog (frisk), a goat (skip and hop), a pony (prance), a donkey (drum), and a capering cow keep adding their rowdy actions to the frog's invitation to dance until they all end up in the cool of the pool. Have your listeners repeat the motion words as they accumulate one by one. Their cues this time will be the pictures of the animals.

4. Read one of the books from the fourth group (sequential patterns). **My Truck Is Stuck** (Lewis, K., 2002, New York: Hyperion) is the hilarious story of two dog drivers who get stuck in a prairie dog hole on the desert with a truckload of bones. They make a big HELP! PLEASE HELP! sign and stop every vehicle that comes along. Tug and tow, two engines roar. But the truck won't go. Not one inch more. First one vehicle hitches up and pulls, then two, three, four, five, and finally a tow truck pulls them out. But by now a parade of sneaky prairie dogs has relieved the truck of every single bone!

Listeners quickly learn to repeat the refrain, adding one more engine each time. In the meantime, have them decipher the signs on the different vehicles and the huge words in LARGE FONT. Here is a predictable book easy to reenact, not with child actors, but with vehicles children retrieve from the block shelves. Line 'em up, hitch 'em on, and pull! If you fill the stuck truck with crackers and let the listeners be sneaky prairie dogs, the truck will soon be empty and the children full!

SUGGESTED READINGS

Bridge, C. A. (1986). Predictable books for beginning readers and writers. In M. R. Sampson (Ed.), *The pursuit of literacy: Early reading and writing*. Dubuque, IA: Kendall/Hunt.

McVicker, C. J. (2007). Young readers respond: The importance of child participation in emerging literacy. *Young Children, 62*(3), 18–22.

Morrow, L. M., Freitag, E., & Gambrell, L. B. (2009). *Using children's literature in preschool to develop comprehension*. 2nd Ed. Newark, DE: International Reading Association.

Strasser, J., & Sephlocha, H. (2007). Using picture books to support young children's literacy. *Childhood Education, 83*(4), 219–224.

Song Storybooks

CONCEPT

One of the most effective ways of making a connection between singing, a right-brain function, and reading, a left-brain function, is through *song storybooks*. Song storybooks are picture books whose stories are told in the words of children's favorite songs. Such books are predictable because children already know the words of the songs by heart. Now they are able to see them illustrated in pictures and in print. What fun! A line from the song is illustrated on each page with pictures of the song characters enacting what the words describe. Most of these books have the musical notations on the front or back pages. Children are delighted to see a song they know in the pages of a book. Can they recognize any of the printed words?

Jalongo and Ribblett (1997) say: "When children participate in read aloud/sing aloud sessions with song picture books, they are involved in authentic, holistic literacy experiences, rather than task-focused instruction that breaks up reading into discrete skills" (p. 16). Moreover, children have fun participating in the experience both by singing and eventually reading the words, and will want to repeat it. Some of the books you may want your children to experience include those in Figure 42–1. Although tapes or CDs are available for some of the songs, if children know the tune and words, it is more effective for them to sing the songs without musical accompaniment as you turn the book pages.

Activities

*1. Read **Skip to My Lou*** (Westcott, N. B., 1989, Boston: Little, Brown). Here is a traditional song in book form about the farm animals who cause all sorts of mischief in the farmhouse when the farmer is away. The farmer's boy tries to shoo away the "flies in the sugarbowl," but that's just the start of it. There are "cats in the buttermilk," "pigs in the parlor," "cows in the kitchen," "roosters in the pantry," and "sheep in the bathtub," all having a hullabaloo in the riotous illustrations. So what can the poor boy do? Why, join in, of course.

I Love You! A Bushel and a Peck (Wells, R., 2005)

If You're Happy and You Know It (Warhola, J., 2007)

Itsy Bitsy Spider (Toms, K., 2009)

Miss Mary Mack (Hoberman, M., 1998)

On Top of Spaghetti (Johnson, P., 2006)

Over the Rainbow (CD) (Collins, J., 2010)

She'll Be Coming 'round the Mountain (Emmett, J., 2006)

Skip to My Lou (Westcott, N. B., 1989)

Sunshine on My Shoulders (CD) (Denver, J., 2003)

The Wheels on the School Bus (Moore, M., 2006)

FIGURE 42–1 Song Storybooks.

Have your children sing the song without seeing the book until they are familiar with it. Then read the book to one small group at a time. Have them investigate the hilarious hodgepodge of details on every page. How many cats get into the buttermilk? Can anyone find 12? What are the pigs in the parlor up to? And sheep snorkeling in the bathtub? Next, sing the song together as you turn the pages.

Play a circle singing game with the various animals acting out their roles in the center and the rest of the class singing and clapping out the catchy rhythm. At the same time remember that it is the words of the book that are most important in this activity. Can any children put their finger on words like "sugarbowl," "buttermilk," "parlor," or "pantry"? Write these words on cards and have the appropriate animal actors wave them around when it is their turn.

2. One of the favorite song storybooks is sure to be **On Top of Spaghetti** (Johnson, P., 2006, New York: Scholastic). Make sure everyone knows the words and music before reading to one small group at a time. The pictures make all the difference, illustrating the wild story about Yodeler Jones, his Spaghetti Emporium and Musicale, and the Big Sneeze that sends his special meatball hurtling out the door and down the street with everybody chasing it. On the last page readers who pay attention find out who sneezed. Wonderful new words of the story (not the song) should keep the hilarity going (fried fritter fricassee, smack-dab, a-whooshin' and a-whizzin', tadwhacker, boomeranged, mush).

As you reread the story, stop where the story does to have your group sing the first verse of the song, and start when you raise your hand to continue the story. They will need to repeat this verse four times before picking up the final verses of the song at the end. Sound complicated? It is not because children must follow along as you read, helping them to realize it is the words not the pictures that tell the story. Afterwards, it's even more fun to have spaghetti and meatballs for lunch.

3. Read this version of the traditional song **The Wheels on the School Bus** (Moore, M., 2006, New York: HarperCollins). The verses tell what the kids say, the teachers say, the librarian says, the coach says, the nurse says, the lunch ladies say, the music teacher says, the art teacher says, the custodian says, and the driver (who turns out to be the principal) says at the end. Alert listeners can tell who the driver/principal is by the hat he wears.

Read the book several times with small groups singing the words until they know them by heart. Then have children reenact the story/song by taking the parts of the characters. They must each sing/say their words when you signal them. One class wanted to add their own verses because they wanted the characters to say different words. In that case hang name cards around the necks of each character and let them make up their own words when the time comes.

4. Read/sing this rollicking tale of a western girl visitor in **She'll Be Coming 'round the Mountain** (Emmett, J., 2006, New York: Atheneum). Its wacky western art will capture the children's attention, and its cumulative phrases at the end of each verse will get them toe-tapping and clapping. Run your finger under each one of the large-font phrases (Toot-toot! Whoa back! Tee-Hee! Squish-Splat! Yee-Ha! Bish-Bosh! Slurp! Slurp! and Hi, Babe!) that needs to be repeated after every verse. Then open up the swinging doors to a four-page celebration at the end. Can the children remember all the phrases and their order each time? Can you?

There are actions to go with each phrase, too, illustrated at the end of the book, but the children may want to make up their own, as McVicker (2007) tells us: "You will marvel at the uninhibited, spontaneous responses as they react to characters and repeat joyful language" (p. 21). What a painless way to learn phonemic awareness!

SUGGESTED READINGS

Barclay, K. D., & Walver, J. (1992). Linking lyrics and literacy through song picture books. *Young Children, 47*(4), 76–85.

Beaty, J. J., & Pratt, L. (2011). *Early literacy in preschool and kindergarten: A multicultural perspective.* 3rd ed. Boston: Pearson.

Jalongo, M. R., & Ribblett, D. M. (1997). Using song picture books to support emergent literacy. *Childhood Education, 74*(1), 15–28.

McVicker, C. J. (2007). Young readers respond: The importance of child participation in emerging literacy. *Young Children, 62*(3), 18–22.

Vukelich, C., & Christie, J. (2009). *Building a foundation for preschool literacy: Effective instruction for children's reading and writing development.* 2nd ed. Newark, DE: International Reading Association.

Book Characters

CONCEPT

As noted previously, before most young children can "emerge into reading" at the preschool level, they need to develop a "sense of story," that is, that stories are plotted narratives in which characters act in certain ways and events take place in a sequence. The youngest children do not view stories from picture books that way at first. They tend to treat each page of the book as a separate unit, not part of a continuing narrative. The more experience children have with picture book stories and their characters, the more aware they become of this narrative flow.

The more familiar children become with the characters in their favorite stories, the more they begin to make sense of this narrative structure. To make their sense of story even stronger, some teachers have children pretend to be their favorite characters and act out the story. (See Strategy 13, "Story Drama.") In a 1995 study, Kiefer noted that "younger children often chose a character that they wanted to be as they read or looked through a book" (p. 30). Book characters become real for young children. They become models the children may want to emulate.

Another effective way to bring stories and book characters alive is through the use of character cutouts and character dolls. After all, one of the reasons children come to love certain books is because they can identify in some way with the characters. If they can actually play with their favorite characters outside of the book, they will even be able to create their own narratives.

Activities

1. Character cutouts. To make a character cutout, simply scan its picture from the book, cut it out, and laminate it. To make it stand up fasten it to a small piece of foam for a base. Make whole

This child "reads" the story to his llama doll.

families of character cutouts and then children can make up their own stories, perhaps using buildings in the block center or a dollhouse as their characters' houses. If everyone makes a character from a book they can create their own stories together.

*2. Read **Llama Llama Misses Mama** (Dewdney, A. 2009, New York: Viking).* Read this rhyming story to a small group, with one child holding a llama doll. The story takes Llama Llama through his first day at school. He is shy and doesn't talk or join in. Why did his mama leave him? The teacher tries to get him involved with the other animal children, but he hides. Finally when the teacher tells him his mama will be back to get him at the end of the day he begins playing with the others. When his mama returns he goes with her happily but realizes he loves school, too. Read the story without stopping the first time through. Have the children talk about how they felt on their first day of school.

3. Reread story having different children hold the llama doll. Have the child with the doll act out the story as you read. Can he pretend the llama is sleeping, wakes up, eats his breakfast, goes to school, acts shy, tries to hide, and finally plays with the others? If the children ask for a third reading, have the child with the doll give it to another listener. Can this child make the llama doll do other actions throughout the story? Can anyone "read" the story as you turn the pages? Would anyone like to "read" the story to the llama doll? Leave out the book and doll for others to use.

4. Make cutouts of people characters from some of the following books and have children act out their roles when you read the books.

> Bombaloo, **Sometimes I'm Bombaloo** (Vail, R., 2002, New York: Scholastic)
>
> Ladybug Girl, Bumblebee Boy, **Ladybug Girl and Bumblebee Boy** (Soman, D., 2009, New York: Dial)
>
> Mike, **Mike and the Bike** (Ward, M., 2005, Salt Lake City: Cookie Jar)
>
> Sally Jean, **Sally Jean, the Bicycle Queen** (Best, C., 2006, New York: Farrar, Straus, & Giroux)
>
> Silly Sally, **Silly Sally** (Wood, A., 1992, Orlando: FL: Harcourt)
>
> Lola and Charlie, **I Am Too Absolutely Small for School** (Child, D., 2004, Cambidge, MA: Candlewick)
>
> Firefighter, **This Is the Firefighter** (Godwin, L., 2009, New York: Hyperion)
>
> Sam, **Born to Read** (Sierra, J., 2008, New York: Knopf)

5. Make cutouts of cultural characters from your books and have children act out their roles, too, while you read the books. Then have a child "read" the story while another one acts out the role.

> Ahmed, **The Day of Ahmed's Secret** (Heide, F., 1990, New York; Lothrop, Lee & Shepard)
>
> Bo jangles, **Rap a Tap Tap: Here's Bo jangles—Think of That!** (Dillon, L. & D., 2002, New York: Blue Sky Press)
>
> Korean girl, **Bee-bim Bop!** (Park, L., 2005, New York: Clarion)
>
> Juan Bobo, **Juan Bobo Goes to Work** (Montes, M., 2000, New York: HarperCollins)
>
> Luke, **Luke Goes to Bat** (Isadora, R., 2005, New York: Putnam's)
>
> Yoon, **My Name Is Yoon** (Recorvits, H., 2003, New York: Farrar Straus & Giroux)

Be sure to read many books with child characters from different cultures so that your children can come to know these cultural characters by identifying and bonding with them. They will learn about how children like themselves from diverse cultures play, work, eat, dress, and go to school; and how they feel, act, and even "act out." Such cultural book characters provide an especially effective way for children to get to know children from different cultures. Just as important—children from these cultures can be motivated to learn to read when they hear stories about characters from their own cultures. Paperback cultural character books are available from Scholastic. (See Figure 43–1.)

FIGURE 43–1 Cultural Characters Featured in Paperback Books from Scholastic.

Rosalba, *Abuela* (Dorros, A., 1991)

Grace, *Amazing Grace* (Hoffman, 1991

Carlos, *Carlos and the Squash Plant* (Stevens, J., 1993)

Handa, *Handa's Surprise* (Browne, E., 1994)

Dear One, *Mama, Do You Love Me?* (Joose, B., 1991)

Margarita, *Margaret and Margarita* (Reiser, L., 1993)

Silvia, *New Shoes for Silvia* (Hurwitz, J., 2003)

Cassie, *Tar Beach* (Ringgold, F., 1991)

Maria, *Too Many Tamales* (Soto, G., 1993)

SUGGESTED READINGS

Beaty, J. J., & Pratt, L. (2011). *Early literacy in preschool and kindergarten: A multicultural perspective.* 3rd ed. Boston: Pearson.

Genishi, C., & Dyson, A. H. (2009). *Children, language, and literacy: Diverse learners in diverse times.* New York: Teachers College Press.

Gillanders, C., & Castro, D. C. (2011). Storybook reading for young dual language learners. *Young Children*, 66(1), 91–95.

Kiefer, B. Z. (1995). *The potential of picturebooks: From visual literacy to aesthetic understanding.* Upper Saddle River, NJ: Merrill/Prentice Hall.

Roser, N. L., & Matines, M. G. (2005). *What a character! Character study as a guide to literary meaning making in grades K–8.* Newark, DE: International Reading Association.

Sound Words

CONCEPT

Sound words are words that describe sounds: sounds made by animals, by vehicles, by objects, or by people. Sound words are important in children's development of phonemic awareness. For this particular strategy, you should be looking for books that have one or two words describing sounds like these: Gr-r-r-r for a growl, cluck-cluck for a hen, snip for scissors, boom for a bass drum, or similar words. Children enjoy making these sounds when you come to the place in a book where they occur. Even more important is the fact that children may be able to identify the words themselves when they come to them in a book.

Identifying words and saying them is at the very core of learning to read. Look through your library to see if any of your picture books are full of sound words. Sometimes the title will suggest that the story uses these words. Next time you purchase books, be sure some of them include sound words like the books in Figure 44–1.

Activities

*1. Read **Looking for a Moose** (Root, P., 2006, Cambridge, MA: Candlewick Press). The four multi-ethnic children who are out on a hike looking for a moose make different sounds in the different

This boy is making the sound of a drum.

FIGURE 44–1 Books with
Sound Words.

> *Boom Boom Go Away!* (Geringer, L., 2010)
>
> *Clip Clop* (Smee, N., 2006)
>
> *Clink, Clank, Clunk!* (Aroner, M., 2006)
>
> *Do You Do a Didgeridoo?* (Page, N., 2008)
>
> *Hush! A Thai Lullaby** (Minfong Ho, H., 1996)
>
> *Looking for a Moose** (Root, P., 2006)
>
> *Polar Bear, Polar Bear, What Do You Hear?* (Martin, B., 1991)
>
> *Summer Beat* (Franco, B., 2007)
>
> *Thump, Quack, Moo: A Whacky Adventure* (Cronin, D., 2008)
>
> *Who Is Driving?* (Timmers, L., 2007)
>
> _____
> *Multicultural.

places they search. In the woods they *tromp stomp*; in the swamp they *squeech, squooch*; in the bushes they *scritch, scratch*; and on the hillside they *trip, trop*. But they don't find a moose until the closest moose makes its own sound: *oo-roog!*

Have your children say these words when you come to them as you read the story. Run your finger under these large-font sound words so children sitting close can see them. Can they make up their own sounds with their hands and feet? What about bugling the moose's call using their hands for a horn? Some listeners will no doubt want to bugle for every moose that pops out from behind the rocks! Let them do it. It will help to make the book a favorite and the sound words unforgettable.

2. Read **Summer Beat** (Franco, B., 2007, New York: Margaret McElderry Books). A little girl and boy ride a skateboard (*clickety-clack*), play in a sprinkler (*shhh, shhh*), swing in a hammock (*swish, swoosh*), watch leaves (*rustle, rustle*), see a bumblebee (*bizzle-bzzz*), hear the raindrops (*pat a tat tat*), eat a burger (*sizzle, sizzle*), lick their fingers (*slup, slup*), eat corn on the cob (*chump, chump*) and chips (*crackle, crunch*), and spit out watermelon seeds (*fwit, fwit*), run a three-legged race (*tha-thump, tha-thump*), light sparklers (*zip, hisss, dz, hissss*), ride their bikes (*flappity, flap*), and watch fireworks (*bam, pop, tzooo, bang, zeeee, bam bam, foooo boom, poppity-crack!*) on the Fourth of July. What a riotous cacophony of sounds!

Read this to a small group, making the sounds yourself. Go through the story again and have them repeat any of these sound words they remember. When children are familiar with the story and the words, have each child in your group choose a sound word to make when you come to it in your reading. Finally, on another day, read the book to a child on either side of you. Can they put their fingers on any of the sound words you read?

3. Read **Hush! A Thai Lullaby** (Minfong Ho, H., 1996, New York: Orchard Books). Read to individuals or pairs who will sit close enough to see the action in this unusual book. A Thai mother tries to hush the animals' sounds around her thatched house while her baby is sleeping in a woven hammock. *TUK-GHAA* peeps the long-tailed lizard, *JEED-JEED* squeaks the fat gray mouse, *UUT-UUT* sniffles the muddy pig, *JIAK-JIAK* cries the loose-limbed monkey, *MAAAU* says the water buffalo, and *HOOM-PRAA* shrieks the elephant. But each time the text shows the mother shushing an animal because her baby's sleeping, the illustrations show the baby sneaking here and there behind the mother's back. Finally everyone is asleep but baby in his hammock, playing with his toes. As you say these strange sound words, put your finger under them and have your listeners repeat the sounds.

4. Read **Polar Bear, Polar Bear, What Do You Hear?** (Martin, B., & Carle, E., 1991, New York: Holt). Read this rhyming predictable book to a small group for a shared reading experience. It is available as both a regular size and big book. Large double-page pictures of a polar bear, lion, hippo, flamingo, zebra, boa constrictor, elephant, leopard, peacock, and walrus each hear the next animal

roaring, snorting, fluting, braying, hissing, trumpeting, snarling, yelping, and bellowing. Finally, on the last page the zookeeper hears children making all these sounds. Children may not know the meaning of the sound words, but they will enjoy making up each of these sounds.

Have children make and color headbands with animal ears for each of the animals. They can wear them every time you read the book. Run your finger under the lines of the big book as you read it. Have children repeat the lines they know in unison. When you come to a sound word, have the children with that animal's headband make the sound. Another time, point to a word that says the name of an animal to see who knows it. Picture clues should help.

SUGGESTED READINGS

Beaty, J. J., & Pratt, L. (2011). *Early literacy in preschool and kindergarten: A multicultural perspective.* 3rd ed. Boston: Pearson.

Hohman, M. (2002). *Fee, fi, phonemic awareness: 130 prereading activities for preschoolers.* Ypsilanti, MI: HighScope Press.

Neuman, S. B., & Roskos, K. A. (1993). *Language and literacy learning in the early years: An integrated approach.* Fort Worth, TX: Harcourt.

Syllables

■ CONCEPT

An important concept in children's learning to read is their recognition of *phonological awareness*: that spoken language is made up of words and syllables. Syllables are the individual sounds in words, the *phonemes*. Phonemic awareness is thus the ability to recognize that spoken words are made up of these sounds. Wasik (2001) tells us: "Children who know how to manipulate sounds in words at an early age have greater success in learning to read in the 1st and 2nd grades" (p. 129).

This is not *phonics,* but instead the oral recognition of sounds in words. Young children can be aware of sounds without knowing the letter name for the sound. For instance, children who recognize words that rhyme or words that begin the same are demonstrating phonemic awareness. Breaking words into separate syllables and combining syllables into words (blending) is the next step (Vukelich & Christie, 2009, pp.12–13).

Children seem to hear rhyming words and alliteration first. Next comes the ability to hear, blend, and isolate individual sounds in words (Opitz, 2000, p. 11). This ability is more caught than taught for most children. Children need to experience a rich classroom environment that includes reading aloud, storytelling, singing, chanting, nursery rhymes, and all kinds of word play. Play with breaking words into syllables helps to promote children's phonemic awareness, the recognition that words are made up of sounds.

The experiences you arrange to help children learn to segment words into their separate sounds should first of all be fun and not isolated drill activities. They should be a part of your everyday oral literacy activities. Clapping, drumming, and rhythmic activities are especially well suited to helping children recognize syllables orally.

Children enjoy clapping out names.

Activities

1. Name-clapping. At morning circle time, go around the circle asking each child to say his or her name while the rest listen carefully. You may have to ask, "Say it again, Brandon. Okay. Did everyone hear the two sounds in Brandon's name? Bran-don? Let's say and clap Brandon's name: Bran-don!

Who's next? Yes, Jessica. Say your name slowly, Jessica, and let's listen for the sounds in your name. Jes-si-ca. How many sounds? Yes, three sounds. Let's say and clap Jessica's name."

Once you have clapped out everyone's name, you can have the children say "hello" to each child by clapping hel-lo and then their name. See if you can trick anyone by pointing to children here and there instead of in order.

Finally, have children clap out the syllables of each name without saying the name. Good. Now you can be the clapper and try to trick them again. Clap once without saying a name and ask them whose name you just clapped. "Does anyone recognize Mark?" Clap three times. "Whose name is that? Yes, Jes-si-ca, but also Jer-em-y, Greg-or-y, La-shan-dra, and Sa-man-tha." Clap two times. "Does anyone recognize Ma-son or Jef-frey or Kay-la or Me-gan or Ke-shawn?" Clap four times. "Who can that be? What about An-ton-i-o or Al-ex-an-der or San-ti-a-go?" Once children catch on, they will all want to take turns being the name-clapper at circle time every day.

2. Dinosaur name-clapping. Children seem to have a fascination with dinosaurs. Not only do they like to see pictures of these great beasts in their books or play with toy dinos in the block center, but they love to hear their names pronounced. Get out your dinosaur books for some terrific name-clapping. In **Saturday Night at the Dinosaur Stomp** (Shields, C., 1997, Cambridge, MA: Candlewick Press), the dinosaurs all gather for their annual bash. *Ple-si-o-saur-us* paddles in. A *pter-o-dac-tyl* family flies in. A *pro-to-cer-a-tops* brings her eggs. *Dip-lo-doc-us* plods on big fat legs. Mama *mai-a-saur* brings her babies. *I-guan-o-don* shouts. *An-kyl-o-saur-us* drums. *Pen-ta-cer-a-tops* performs. *Ty-ran-no-saur-us* Rex leads a conga line. Even you will be learning how to pronounce these tongue twisters when you all clap out the dinosaur names.

If the children are interested, follow up with a story reenactment. Children can make their own dinosaur heads with paper bags. You can print the hyphenated names of the creatures on cards to be worn around the necks of the actors. Now the children can see for themselves what dinosaur names look like when separated into syllables to help them pronounce the names. Converting spoken sounds into written word segments helps children understand more about how speech is converted into writing. Have the actors dance up a storm to a tape or CD with a strong beat.

Some children are sure to want to draw or paint pictures of the dinosaurs. When you or they label their pictures, be sure to hyphenate the names so children can see the syllables. Some children will want to see their own names written in hyphenated syllables like this, too. They may also want to make up their own stories about the Dinosaur Stomp, featuring the character they represented.

3. Other fine books for dinosaur name-clapping are **Harry and the Dinosaurs Say "Raahh!"** (Whybrow, I., 2001, New York: Random House) and **Harry and the Dinosaurs Go to School** (Whybrow, I., 2006, New York: Random House). In **Harry and the Dinosaurs Say "Raahh!"** the boy and his dinosaurs go to the dentist, and in **Harry and the Dinosaurs Go to School** Harry takes his dinosaurs to his first day of school. Harry actually calls out the names of the dinosaurs: Apatosaurus, Anchisaurus, Scelidosaurus, Triceratops, Tyrannosaurus, Pterodactyl, and Stegosaurus, so your children will have the fun of saying these names over and over. Both books can make exciting story reenactments. What else can you do with dinosaurs?

SUGGESTED READINGS

Opitz, M. F. (2000). *Rhymes & reasons: Literature and language play for phonological awareness.* Portsmouth, NH: Heinemann.

Roskos, K. A., Christie, J. F., & Richgels, D. J. (2003). The essentials of early literacy instruction. *Young Children, 58*(2), 52–59.

Vukelich, C., & Christie, J. (2009). *Building a foundation for preschool literacy: Effective instruction for children's reading and writing development.* 2nd ed. Newark, DE: International Reading Association.

Wasik, B. L. (2001). Phonemic awareness and young children. *Childhood Education, 77*(3), 128–133.

46 Kindergarten Reading

CONCEPT

The kindergarten year can be an exciting one for young children either emerging into reading on their own or ready for adult direct instruction. The classroom itself should remind the children of their preschool with learning centers full of fascinating activities, shelves with toys and tools, and walls bright with posters, children's drawings, and paintings. Environmental print should fill the three main types of centers found in many kindergarten classrooms: Literacy Center, Discovery or Exploration Center, and Dramatic Play Center. All three of these large areas will be involved in early literacy.

A favorite site is sure to be the Literacy Center with its Reading Corner and Writing Spot. The Reading Corner may feature an upholstered chair or sofa with soft cushions, colorful beanbag chairs, oversized floor pillows, a book nook or reading loft for independent readers, puppets and character dolls, and of course a generous supply of the latest picture books on shelves or a carousel or clipped with kitchen clips to a rainbow of dangling ribbons, and a listening area with headsets and tape/CD deck. Research has shown that children who have access to books in the classroom read up to 50 percent more than students in classrooms without libraries (Rog, 2001, p. 40).

But wait! This looks more like a preschool classroom, doesn't it? How is kindergarten reading different from that in preschool? The difference lies not in what it looks like but in what happens in it. The most common kindergarten reading types are:

1. Interactive storybook reading (read-alouds and read-alongs)
2. Shared reading
3. Independent reading

A teacher demonstrates to a small group how a book works.

Read-Alouds

Read-alouds are most often done with larger groups than in preschool. Frequently the total class gathers around the teacher to listen to the book. It is a carefully planned activity for building vocabulary, helping children develop an understanding of story structure, and encouraging higher-level thinking. Books with action-oriented plots, rich language, plenty of dialogue, a main character children can identify with, and a satisfying ending are the best books to use. The Charlie and Lola books mentioned previously (see Strategies 5, 14, 22, 35, and 43) fulfill these criteria, plus they are funny, children love them—and Lola always wins (even when she doesn't)!

For example, the book **But Excuse Me That Is My Book** (Child, D., 2005, New York: Dial) gets listeners excited from the start when they hear that little Lola is going to the library to borrow *Beetles, Bugs, and Butterflies* yet *again*, because it is the best book in the whole world, very great, and extremely very interesting. But she can't find it. Big brother Charlie tries to interest her in a different book, but they have too many big words and not enough pictures—and there goes a girl with Lola's book! Oh, no!

The teacher will plan in advance to read the dialogue between Charlie and Lola in different voices. She will also plan to allow children to make comments or ask questions throughout the story. Finally, she plans to stop before the ending to ask the listeners how they think the story will end. Does anyone guess that Lola will end up deciding that Charlie's *Cheetahs and Chimpanzees* is the most best book in the whole wide world?

The vocabulary words *borrow, obviously, chariots,* and *encyclopedia* can be written on cards for the children to hold when they come to those words at future readings. Books like this will be read again and again, not only for the children's enjoyment, but for them to experience *mastery* of stories and reading, the second of the 3-Ms of self-discovery. (See Strategy 19, "Alphabet.")

Read-Alongs

Read-alongs occur when teachers demonstrate to a small group at a time how a book works. Each child in the group holds the same book in her hand. Sets of books from educational supply companies include kits of four copies of each paperback along with a CD narrating the text word-for-word. (See Figure 46–1.) As the teacher reads her book to a small group, each child holds the same book and is encouraged to follow along. They are not actually reading, but beginning to learn that the words the teacher is saying occur in the same lines in their books. Teachers must pay close attention to how the children are handling their books to see if they are on the right page and right line. The CD for each set of books can be used for independent read-alongs. Children wear headsets and listen to the story on their own while trying to follow along in their book. (See Strategy 4, "Listening Center.")

Shared Reading

In shared reading teachers often read from big books to demonstrate the use of reading strategies. (See Strategy 40, "Big Books.") They choose books with simple, repetitive language and illustrations that match the text. The print is large enough for the group to see, with only one or two lines per page. The

Set 4	Set 3
Goodnight Moon	*The Doorbell Rang*
The Three Billy Goats Gruff	*Make Way for Ducklings*
It Looked Like Spilt Milk	*If the Dinosaurs Came Back*
Five Little Monkeys Jumping on the Bed	*Caps for Sale*

FIGURE 46–1   Sets of Small Group Read-Alongs from Lakeshore (1-800-778-4456).

teachers may use a "reading wand" to track lines of text or point out certain words. After reading the story the teacher will go back, asking the children to look for certain words: words that rhyme, that begin with the same letter, or have matching initial sounds. Children may be asked to substitute words for words in the text.

Independent Reading

Independent reading time may occur daily when everyone in the class is asked to find a book and read, whether or not they can actually read. Instead, most will flip the pages of several books or spend time looking at the pictures. Other children may make up their own stories using the pictures in the book. They may do "pretend reading," talking about the pictures as they turn the pages. Children who are actually beginning to read often verbalize aloud as they read. Eventually, most will improve whatever it is they are doing.

Some will be discouraged that they can't actually read when they discover that pretend reading is not real reading. Martinez and Teale (1988) found that "when children selected classroom Big Books, they were more likely to try to read conventionally." In fact, all children in most classes that encourage independent reading will begin to read conventionally before the end of the school year (Rog, 2001, p. 66).

Activities

1. Reading around the room. Even if they can't read books, most children will find that they can read words during a reading around the room activity. Give each child some kind of pointer (chopstick, ruler, back scratcher) for tracking words they find as they travel around the room looking for environmental print. When they find a word they can read, they or you can copy it on a card to be kept in a box in their cubby.

2. Plan a read-aloud activity. Choose one of Doreen Child's Charlie and Lola books to be read aloud. Go through the book deciding where to pause for children's comments and your questions, vocabulary words to look for, and follow-up activities to pursue in different learning centers.

SUGGESTED READINGS

Martinez, M., & Teale, W. (1988). Reading in a kindergarten classroom library. *The Reading Teacher, (40),* 444–451.

Parker, A., & Neuharth-Pritchett, S. (2006). Developmentally appropriate practice in kindergarten: Factors shaping teacher beliefs and practice. *Journal of Research in Childhood Education, 21*(1), 65–78.

Reyes, C. L. (2010). A teacher's case for learning center extensions in kindergarten. *Young Children, 65*(5), 94–98.

Rog, L. J. (2001). *Early literacy instruction in kindergarten.* Newark, DE: International Reading Association.

Literacy Bags

CONCEPT

Literacy bags, sometimes called "bookbags," "book packs," or "book backpacks," are containers holding paperback books along with book extension props and activities such as puppets, dolls, character cutouts, a book audiotape or CD, and an activities sheet for parents. Literacy bags are intended for home use. It is important that parents become aware of their children's literacy activities in school and give support and encouragement at home. Morrow, Freitag, and Gambrell (2009) feel that parents should definitely read to their children at home: "When parents interact with their children during storybook reading, they define words, repeat information, and explain ideas, enhancing children's literacy development" (p. 86).

When you talk to parents, explain to them the benefits of reading aloud to children, invite them to watch and participate in classroom read-aloud activities, and finally tell them their children will be bringing home literacy bags with books for them to read to their children. You can develop your own lending library of paperback copies of the same books you are reading in the classroom along with various tapes, CDs, or props. Children can sign out the literacy bags for week-long use. This gives parents enough time to listen to the tape, read the story aloud, talk about the book, and play the activities with their children. Meier (2000), lists the following advantages for using literacy bags in the home:

- Helps children develop a strong sense of self and independence in school literacy.
- Recognizes the respect that parents afford teachers.
- Coordinates preschool literacy learning with kindergarten goals and practices.
- Recognizes and builds on the literacy of entire families.
- Shows the variety of child-created literacy practices invented in children's home. (p. 133)

The children are each putting a doll in their book backpacks.

Meier notes what one parent thought about the bookbag program: "'I like the bookbag program because it gave the kids a sense of independence, and Akilah felt proud to have her own book come home. She took care of it, and she wanted to read it as soon as she got home. She wanted to read *her* book'" (p. 133).

Second-language speakers may want to listen to the tape/CD first while looking at book pages. Parents who are not used to reading to their children may want to listen to the tape/CD to gain confidence in their own reading aloud. Neuman (1997) feels that engaging parents and children in mutual activities that include book reading, but are not limited to it, may constitute the richest potential for supporting children's early literacy development (p. 119).

Most parents want to support their children's literacy development but may not know how. The activities sheet that you include in the bookbag can give them suggestions of how to read the story, what questions to ask the children about the story, how to get the children involved in the story reading, and what extension activities they can do.

Activities

1. Make your own literacy bags. Make the packs from large baggies from the supermarket, or backpacks can be purchased from discount stores. If an audiotape or CD of your book is not available, make your own. Include in each literacy bag (in addition to book and audiotape or CD) cutouts of the characters made from page scans from the books, a doll or stuffed animal, a puzzle made from a page scan from the book, two or three crayons and blank paper, and an activities sheet. Find out which families do not have cassette or CD players and provide little hand-held sets for borrowing.

*2. Make an activity sheet for **Mama, Do You Love Me?*** (Joose, B. M., 1991, San Francisco: Chronicle Books).

First, read the book to the child who will be sitting on your lap or close to you. Read it again if the child agrees.

As you reread the story, get the child involved by asking questions.

On the title page, you could ask: "Do you think the little girl loves her mama? How can you tell?"

Turn the page and ask: "Do you think the mama loves her little girl? How can you tell?"

On the next page, you might ask the child to find the raven's treasure, the dog's tail, and the whale's spout.

On the next page, have the child point to the "umiak," the "puffin," and so on through the book.

Play the book tape with the child looking at each page. Help the child turn the page when she hears the signal.

The child can play with the cutout characters (mama, girl, raven, whale, puffin, walrus, and polar bear); she can also trace them and color them. Or include a character doll.

Now ask the child to read the story to you. She may tell you that she can't read, but you can have her read the pictures in the book. (Most children delight in "reading" to their parents. This book should already be familiar to children since they have read it in the classroom, as well.)

Check off which of these activities you did with the child. Write which ones the child especially liked and any other comments you want to make. Read the story several times to the child, asking questions about what's happening in the story, playing the tape of the story, and asking the child to "read" the story to you.

SUGGESTED READINGS

Barbour, A. C. (1998/1999). Home literacy bags: Promote family involvement. *Childhood Education, 75*(2), 71–75.

Beaty, J. J., & Pratt, L. (2011). *Early literacy in preschool and kindergarten: A multicultural perspective.* 3rd ed. Boston: Pearson.

Dever, M. T., & Burts, D. C. (2002). Using family literacy bags to enhance family involvement. *Dimensions of Early Childhood, 30*(1), 16–20.

Meier, D. R. (2000). *Scribble scrabble: Learning to read and write.* New York: Teachers College Press.

Morrow, L. M., Freitag, E., & Gambrell, L. B. (2009). *Using children's literature in preschool to develop comprehension.* 2nd ed. Newark, DE: International Reading Association.

Neuman, S. B. (1997). Guiding young children's participation in early literacy development: A family literacy program for adolescent mothers. *Early Child Development and Care*, 127–128.

Webs

CONCEPT

Curriculum webs are devices that assist an early childhood staff in planning learning activities based on a particular theme. Each web is a format for capturing a theme-based curriculum idea as it emerges during brainstorming sessions with the staff and children. Such webs allow the staff to design a program based on appropriate learning goals, interests, and ideas as they occur. The curriculum in many early childhood programs has usually been a previously designed overall educational plan based on an academic subject that the teacher must follow.

In contrast, curriculum webs are often constructed on the spot and respond to current classroom happenings. Such webs are the basis for an *emergent curriculum* that responds to both the staff's and the children's interests and needs. As Jones and Nimmo (1994) point out in *Emergent Curriculum,* "In early childhood education, curriculum isn't the focus, children are . . . Curriculum is *what happens* in an educational environment—not what is rationally planned to happen" (p. 12).

In a classroom concerned with young children's emergent literacy, such webs will necessarily consist of ideas and activities that support children's development of speaking, listening, reading, and writing skills. The webs presented here evolved from a staff's and children's passionate interest in a particular picture book in use because of a classroom issue it addressed.

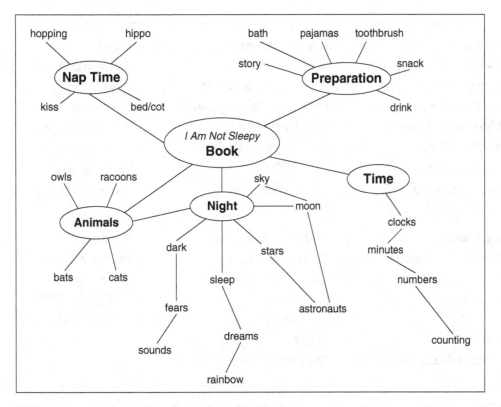

FIGURE 48–1   Web Based on the Book *I Am NOT Sleepy.*

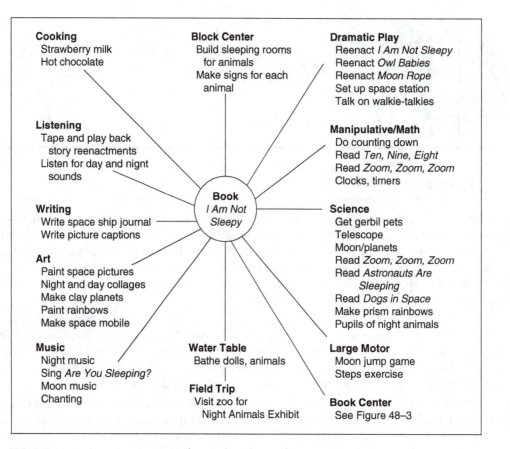

Cooking
Strawberry milk
Hot chocolate

Block Center
Build sleeping rooms
   for animals
Make signs for each
   animal

Dramatic Play
Reenact *I Am Not Sleepy*
Reenact *Owl Babies*
Reenact *Moon Rope*
Set up space station
Talk on walkie-talkies

Listening
Tape and play back
   story reenactments
Listen for day and night
   sounds

Manipulative/Math
Do counting down
Read *Ten, Nine, Eight*
Read *Zoom, Zoom, Zoom*
Clocks, timers

Book
I Am Not Sleepy

Writing
Write space ship journal
Write picture captions

Science
Get gerbil pets
Telescope
Moon/planets
Read *Zoom, Zoom, Zoom*
Read *Astronauts Are*
   Sleeping
Read *Dogs in Space*
Make prism rainbows
Pupils of night animals

Art
Paint space pictures
Night and day collages
Make clay planets
Paint rainbows
Make space mobile

Music
Night music
Sing *Are You Sleeping?*
Moon music
Chanting

Water Table
Bathe dolls, animals

Large Motor
Moon jump game
Steps exercise

Field Trip
Visit zoo for
   Night Animals Exhibit

Book Center
See Figure 48–3

FIGURE 48–2   Learning Center Web Based on the Book *I Am NOT Sleepy*.

Preparation

Close Your Eyes

Goodnight Moon

Ten, Nine, Eight

10 Minutes till Bedtime

Kiss Good Night

The House at Night

Night Shift Daddy

Fear of the Dark

A Beasty Story

Boo! Made You Jump!

Francis the Scaredy Cat

"I'm Not Scared!"

The Owl Who Was Afraid
   of the dark

Boo to You!

Moon

Astronauts Are Sleeping

Crab Moon

Dogs in Space

The Moon over Star

Moon Rope

On the Moon

Hedgie Blasts Off!

Time/Clocks

10 Minutes till Bedtime

Ten, Nine, Eight

I Am Not Sleepy

Night Animals

Bats at the Library

Bats at the Beach

Crab Moon

Owl Babies

Stellaluna

Francis the Scaredy Cat

Sounds

Roar of a Snore

The Sound of Day, the
   Sound of Night

Hush! A Thai Lullaby

Dreams

Maisy's Rainbow Dream

FIGURE 48–3   Books to Support *I Am Not Sleepy* Activities.

Unit:	**Animals Who Live in the Dark**
Theme:	How can owls fly at night without bumping into things?
Objective:	Children will learn how the large pupils in owls' eyes help them to see at night.
Materials:	A card table and blankets enough to cover it completely; the book: *Owl Babies*; a basket of socks: white and brown; peel-off yellow eye stickers; a black marker; a hand mirror.
Lesson:	Read the story *Owl Babies* to one small group at a time. Have them look at the eyes of the three baby barn owls. Do they notice the very large black pupils of their eyes? Talk about the pupils of eyes being the place where light comes into the eyes so we can see. Have everyone look at their own eyes with the hand mirror. Have them notice the black spot in the eye called a "pupil." When it is bigger, more light comes in. Set up the card table and cover it completely with the blankets. Have one child at a time crawl into this dark space and sit for a while. Talk to the child about what she sees at first. Ask her when she can see more as her eyes get used to the dark. Have her come out and look in the mirror again. Are her pupils larger than before? That means more light can come in and she can see better in the dark—just like the owls. Any child who is afraid to crawl into the dark space may be able to put just his head in under the blanket. If not, don't press the issue.

- Have the children make owl hand puppets with the white socks and yellow peel-off stickers for eyes.
- Have them put pupils in the middle of the yellow eyes with the black marker.
- Reenact the story *Owl Babies* with three white hand puppets for the babies and one brown one for the mother.

Are the mother's pupils larger than the babies? What does this mean?

Follow-up:	Read the book *The Owl Who Was Afraid of the Dark*. Talk about why he might be afraid. How did he get over his fear? Did anyone notice the pupils of the black cat's eyes? What is another meaning for the word "pupil"? Can one word have different meanings?

- Have the children make up their own story about owls.
- Have the children paste a collage of cutout colored paper scraps on black or backing paper.
- Take a trip to the zoo to see the night animals exhibit.
- Have children write in their journals about owls.

FIGURE 48–4 Lesson Plan Example for "Animals Who Live in the Dark."

The children in this all-day program were having trouble settling down after lunch to take an afternoon nap. One of the picture books the teachers happened to discover that spoke so eloquently to this issue was another Charlie and Lola book. This time the book was called ***I am NOT Sleepy and I Will NOT Go to Bed.*** The teachers read it during story time just after lunch to try to settle the children and prepare them for a nap. It worked. The children loved it and wanted it read every day. Afterward, they settled down and took their naps. The teachers wondered: with such intense children's interest, could a book like this serve as the focus for other curriculum activities? Here was an opportunity to use the webbing technique to find out.

The teacher wrote the book title in the middle of a newsprint pad and then asked the children and staff to suggest other ideas about going to sleep that they thought about. After each idea she asked what that reminded them of and drew a line from one idea to another, creating the web shown in Figure 48–1.

Next, the staff studied the web to decide what learning centers could involve children in pursuing these topics. They made a second web, shown in Figure 48–2, listing the learning centers and possible activities. Then they searched through their rather extensive library to see what books might support the topics from the webs and came up with the titles shown in Figure 48–3. Finally they made lesson plans, one at a time, to support the ideas they intended to pursue. (See Figure 48–4.)

Webs like these can help the staff to focus on children's intense interests and translate them into literacy activities in every learning center in the classroom. Most teachers of young children have learned that one thing leads to another in early childhood programs. Using webs can make these "things" visible and help teachers to decide which of the ideas to follow, as well as how to follow them in the lesson plans they create.

Activities

1. Read **Bat Night at the Library** (Lies, 2008). Before reading the book, ask the children what they think the bats might do in the library at night.

What would the children do if they were bats? Make a web from these ideas. Read the book to see if they guessed correctly. Extensions to this activity can include visiting a library or making up a story of what cats might do if they visited the library at night.

SUGGESTED READINGS

Beaty, J. J. (2012). *Skills for preschool teachers.* 9th ed. Columbus, OH: Pearson.

Dizes, D. E., & Dorl, J. (1999). Your mop is my guitar: Emergent curriculum in our classroom. *Young Children, 54*(4), 14–16.

Jones, E., & Nimmo, J. (1994). *Emergent curriculum.* Washington, DC: National Association for the Education of Young Children.

Lewin-Benham, A. (2006). One teacher, 20 preschoolers, and a goldfish: Environmental awareness, emergent curriculum, and documentation. *Young Children, 61*(2), 28–34.

49 Assessing Reading Progress

CONCEPT

Children in early childhood classrooms are in the beginning stages of learning to read. As they participate in the playful learning activities you have set up and the book reading and storytelling you have arranged, they begin their emergence into reading. For you to understand their progress in this emergence, it is important for you to look at each child separately. Learning to read is a complex process that each child approaches individually. Although reading accomplishments can be listed chronologically, not every child progresses in this order, some skip certain steps altogether, and some emerge into reading through writing. Thus, it is essential that you view children's progress one child at a time and that you use several different assessment techniques.

Most of the assessments that early childhood educators use are informal. According to Vukelich and Christie (2009), "Informal assessments are typically called *authentic assessments* because these data are gathered while children engage in everyday classroom activities and real-life literacy tasks" (p. 84). They also describe the International Reading Association's statement: "Early reading and writing cannot simply be measured as a set of narrowly defined skills on standardized tests. These measures often are not reliable or valid indicators of what children can do in typical practice; nor are they sensitive to language variations, culture, or experiences of young children" (pp. 84–85).

The assessment of children's reading behaviors in the classroom can be accomplished in a number of other ways:

- Ongoing observations using logs and developmental checklists
- Analysis of children's art and writing products
- Videotaping and audiotaping children at work and play
- Individual interviews

Interviewing children about a favorite book helps teachers learn about children's reading progress.

Why Assess Reading Behaviors?

It is important to learn where each child stands in his progress of emergence into literacy in order to plan appropriate activities that will support this development. If you find that many of the children have never had experience with books before, you will want to work with small groups doing book-holding and page-turning games. Daily reading to small groups and individuals should be your most important activity. Bringing children together with books should be your goal. A selection of highly attractive picture books and their accompanying character dolls, cutouts, puppets, or stuffed animals should be available to the children, with each book being a lead-in to various classroom activities. (See Strategy 48, "Webs.") Literacy bags with paperback versions of classroom books can be sent home with the children.

As soon as children and books truly come together, the children's reading behaviors will change. Thus it is important to keep up your assessment of their accomplishments as an ongoing process. If you find after several months that many of them have not yet developed a "sense of story," you will want to set up activities that help them understand how stories evolve in a sequence of events. Story drama, predictable books, and book characters should support this growth. A book buddy who already knows what a story is can be paired with a child who hasn't caught on yet.

Pressure to learn should not be applied to anyone, and failure to understand should never be criticized. Children learn at their own speed and in their own good time. Your job is to make books and reading so attractive everyone will want to get involved in the stimulating activities you provide. All the children can take part in every activity. Even accomplished book handlers can participate in the small group that is playing page-turning games. Accomplished story retellers can add immensely to the small group that is still trying to make sense of a story.

But Enz and Morrow (2009) remind us that one measure alone cannot be the sole source for evaluating a child's progress. Multiple assessment tools such as checklists, interviews, anecdotal records, and daily performance samples must be done frequently to show the whole picture (p. 8).

Activities

1. Start with a reading behaviors checklist. Using the checklist in Figure 49–1 to assess each child's reading behaviors is a good way for you to learn the reading behaviors yourself, so you will know

FIGURE 49–1 Reading Behaviors Checklist.

Name_____ Age_____
Observers_____ Dates_____

_____Holds book right side up
_____Starts with first page
_____Turns pages right to left
_____Looks through book carefully without skipping pages
_____Does pretend reading
_____Labels objects in pictures (story not formed)
_____Treats each page as a separate unit
_____Tells story by naming pictures
_____Understands story is a sequence of events
_____Retells story through memorization
_____Retells story using key story elements
_____Recognizes that print tells the story
_____Does finger-point reading of some words
_____Is preoccupied with word recognition
_____Reads print more fluently

what to look for and expect in the future. The checklist is also helpful for you to determine what activities need to be set up as children progress in their development over time. This is a developmental checklist describing children's progress and not a list of behaviors that children must accomplish step-by-step, or at all. Some children may have accomplished only a few items. Not many 3- and 4-year-olds will accomplish all of them in preschool. You may also want to keep a daily or weekly log of a child's progress as you note it during the day. This will help you to plan appropriate activities for the child.

2. Analyze children's art and writing products. To determine whether children have developed a "sense of story," look at the series of dated picture stories (caption pictures) a child has done that you have collected and placed in her portfolio. Do the pictures or captions tell a fully formed story with characters and action, or do the captions mainly label the items in the pictures without forming a story? Check other writing products, such as the child's journal, to see whether a story has been formed. For example, the picture by a 4-year-old girl shown in Figure 49–2 does not exhibit a sense of story because the girl is only describing the items in her picture.

In contrast, the caption for the picture by a 4-year-old boy shown in Figure 49–3 suggests that he is beginning to understand what a story is about. He tells what is happening and not just what the object is in the picture.

3. Analyze a videotape or audiotape of a child's reading activities, storytelling, or role-playing in dramatic play. As you look or listen to the tapes, can you tell if the child is telling a fully formed story with characters and action or mainly naming things? Is there a narrative with a plot? A beginning, middle, and ending? Sometimes the leader in a dramatic play episode has a story in mind. You may be able to tell this if he directs the other players in what they are supposed to do and say. Most dramatic play episodes, however, unfold on-the-spot without much preplanning. Still, you can talk to the players afterward asking them what they were doing and why.

4. Do individual interviews of the children. Neuman and Roskos (1993) say that interviews with children work best when they resemble friendly conversations (p. 258). Because you want the child to respond to your questions giving specific information, sometimes it is helpful to engage the child in an activity that you then ask him to explain. You might have him draw a picture of his favorite learning center, asking him why he likes it or what he does there. Or you might ask him about a favorite book that you can get from the book center, then asking him to point out his favorite character or anything else he likes about the story. Holding and talking about a favorite toy is another way to elicit information from a child in a friendly, informal manner.

Remember, assessment of children's reading progress is being done for you to be able to set up appropriate reading activities for individuals, groups, and the total class.

FIGURE 49–2 My garden with goodies and vegetables.

FIGURE 49–3   I'm flying
in my banana plane to see
the doctor.

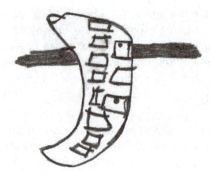

SUGGESTED READINGS

Beaty, J. J., & Pratt, L. (2011). *Early literacy in preschool and kindergarten: A multicultural perspective.* 3rd
   ed. Boston: Pearson.

Enz, B. J., & Morrow, L. M. (2009). *Assessing preschool literacy development: Informal and formal
   measures to guide instruction.* Newark, DE: International Reading Association.

Morrow, L. M., Freitag, E., & Gambrell, L. B. (2009). *Using children's literature in preschool to develop
   comprehension.* 2nd ed. Newark, DE: International Reading Association.

Neuman, S. B., & Roskos, K. A. (1993). *Language and literacy learning in the early years: An integrated
   approach.* Fort Worth, TX: Harcourt.

Vukelich, C., & Christie, J. (2009). *Building a foundation for preschool literacy: Effective instruction for
   children's reading and writing development.* 2nd ed. Newark, DE: International Reading Association.

50 Words, Words, Words

CONCEPT

Words, words, words—what children say, what children hear you say, what children write, what they see written. No matter how you look at it, emergent literacy involves words. To become literate, children need to learn all about words. What have your children learned about words from the strategies you have used with them from this text?

- Can your children identify many words?
- Do they understand that words are made up of letters?
- Do they know that groups of letters make up sounds?
- Are they aware that the words in a picture book tell the story?
- Can they recognize rhyming words?
- What words sound alike to them?
- What "sound words" do they know?
- Do they know any angry words? Any funny words?
- What words can they write?
- What words can they spell?
- What words can they read?
- What words can they read on signs?
- What is their favorite word?

How can you find out? By now you realize that young children learn best through play. Children already know this fact and begin playing with anything new almost immediately. Playing with words should be no trouble at all for them, but it will be up to you to set up playful activities that teach them

This girl says her dinosaur can "twirl" through the wires with its long neck.

new words and new concepts about words. You can have word hunts, word treasure chests, word beanbag, secret words, word surprises, word smelling contests, word missing contests, word eating contests, water word contests, sand word contests, word day contests—and on and on. Here are a few. How children play these games tells you what they have learned about words.

Activities

1. Word hunt. Names are words that children soon recognize, thus it is more meaningful for them to begin with names. Animal names may be easier at first to recognize than other children's names, so start this game with a card on which you have printed the name of each animal you have in your block building center. Start with short names at first, and set out the animals on a table for one of your small groups: cat, dog, horse, cow, pig, sheep—not too many. Hold up each card, say the name, and have the children place it in front of the correct animal. Now shuffle the cards and try again. Can any of the children say the name on the card? Do this until they really know the names.

Now it is time for the word hunt. Take the cards and place them here and there in the block center. Don't make them too hard to find. Stand up the horse and ask the small group to find the name of this animal. Once they have found the correct card, put out another animal and have them find its name.

Another variant of this game is a word hunt with animal puppets. Use big mouth jungle puppets (monkey, rhino, giraffe, alligator, panda, tiger) and hide their name cards in a different learning center. Have each child in your group of six choose and wear a puppet that will have to find its name card. This may be more difficult because the names are longer. Another day, have five children's names on the cards and have the children hide here and there around the room. The sixth child can choose one name card and try to find its owner. Another day, bring out some of the children's favorite animal books and see who can find a word in a book that matches one of the word cards or one of the animal pictures. (See Figure 50–1.)

2. Word smelling contest. Do words actually smell? They do when you write a word representing a smell on a card and then place it in a bag along with its smell (for instance, sweet, sour, lemon, onion, chocolate). Open the bag slightly and let one child at a time take a sniff. Once they have identified the smell, pull out the word and let them hold it. The lemon bag can hold two words: sour and lemon. Mix up the bags and let each child try to identify which one her word came from. Put the cards back in the bags and play it again.

Alligator Baby (Munsch, R., 1997)

Art and Max (Wiesner, D., 2010)

Bats in the Library (Lies, B., 2008)

Chick 'n' Pug (Sattler, J., 2010)

Dinosaurumpus! (Mitton, T., 2002)

Down by the Cool of the Pool (Mitton, T., 2001)

Drat That Fat Cat! (Thompson, P., 2003)

Duck on a Bike (Shannon, D., 2002)

Giggle, Giggle, Quack (Cronin, D., 2002)

Giraffes Can't Dance (Andreae, G., 1999)

Grumpy Gloria (Dewdney, A., 2006)

Llama Llama Misses Mama (Dewdney, A., 2009)

Looking for a Moose (Root, P., 2006)

Tony Baloney (Ryan, P., 2011)

Zachary Z. Packrat (Bessesen, B., 2008)

FIGURE 50–1 Favorite Animal Books.

3. Word eating contest. Make cookie dough in the cooking center. Then put out short-name animal cards and help children to form letters from the dough to spell the animal name. Put them in the oven to bake and eat.

4. Water word contest. Choose one of the children's favorite books and create a series of word games around it. For instance, one class simply loved the silly words and actions from the book *Down by the Cool of the Pool* (Mitton, T., 2002, New York: Scholastic). So the teacher decided to start her word games in the book center with a group of ten children and then move over to the water table. As she read the story, she brought out the animal character mentioned and gave each one to a child to hold: frog, duck, pig, sheep, cat, dog, goat, pony, donkey, and cow. Each of these animals makes its own move in the story:

Frog—dance	Cat—bound	Pony—prance
Duck—flap	Dog—frisk	Donkey—drum
Pig—wiggle	Goat—skip	Cow—caper
Sheep—stamp		

Then she read the story again and had each child make his animal move. Any move would do. Next time through, they all stood around the water table while the teacher read the story. After each toy animal made its move, the child could toss it into the water table (the pool). After everyone had calmed down and returned to the book center, the teacher challenged each animal holder to find the WORD on the page she was reading that told how their animal moved. Most of the movements are in large-font print, children soon discovered.

5. Sand word contest. Ideas like this can apply to any book the children like. Some are sure to want to create a **Dinosaurumpus!** (Mitton, T., 2003, New York: Scholastic) where the different dinosaurs donk, bomp, snip-snap, twist, clatter, rattle, twack, and zoom-zoom. This story can be read around the sand table (the sludgy old swamp) with the children holding toy dinosaurs and having them burrow into the sand after they make their moves. The point of all this bizarre activity is not to teach children to identify funny words, but to help them make the connection of words with sounds, and spoken words with written words. In other words, the goal is to make words *memorable*; then they become *meaningful*. That is what emergent literacy is all about. Let the children themselves help create your next word game. Good "wording" to you and everyone who reads this book!

Appendix

Websites

- Arts Education Partnership
  www.aep-arts.org
- Association for Childhood Education International
  www.acei.org
- Better Brains for Babies
  www.fcs.uga.edu
- Building Blocks
  www.gse.buffalo.edu
- Center on School, Family and Community Partnership
  www.csos.jhu.edu
- Child Care Information Exchange
  www.childcareexchange.com
- Children's Software Online
  www.childrenssoftwareonline.com
- Colorin Colorado (bilingual)
  www.colorincolorado.org.
- Critical Issue: Assessing Young Children's Progress Appropriately
  www.ncrel.org
- Heads Up! Network: National Head Start Association
  www.heads-up.org
- International Reading Association
  www.reading.org
- Kids Source Online
  www.kidsssource.com
- Kidsclick
  www.kidsclick.com
- Ladybug
  www.ladybugmagickids.com
- The Literacy Project
  www.google.com/literacy
- Mother Goose Programs
  www.mothergooseprograms.org
- National Art Education Association
  www.naea-reston.org
- National Association for Bilingual Education
  www.nabe.org
- National Association for the Education of Young Children
  www.naeyc.org

- Read Write Think
  www.readwritethink.org
- Reading Is Fundamental
  www.rif.org
- Reading Rockets
  www.readingrockets.org
- Southern Early Childhood Association
  www.southernearlychildhoodassociation.org
- Start with the Arts
  www.Varts.org
- Teachers and Families
  www.teachersandfamilies.com
- Teaching Strategies
  www.teachingstrategies.org